Paradise Lost: Introduction

THE CAMBRIDGE MILTON FOR
SCHOOLS AND COLLEGES

GENERAL EDITOR: J. B. BROADBENT

Paradise Lost:
Introduction

JOHN BROADBENT
University of East Anglia, Norwich

This is the refrain of a lost age.
Wiping our natural tears
We look unterrified at the dreadful faces
And the flaming sword. Our ears
Are temperd to harsh sounds, and desert places
Blossom with aloes.

RONALD BOTTRALL *Adam unparadised* 1954

Cambridge at the University Press
1972

Published by the Syndics of the Cambridge University Press
Bentley House, 200 Euston Road, London NW1 2DB
American Branch: 32 East 57th Street, New York, N.Y.10022

© Cambridge University Press 1972

Library of Congress Catalogue Card Number: 70–149432

ISBN: hard cover: 0 521 08068 1
paperback: 0 521 09639 1

Printed in Great Britain
at the University Printing House, Cambridge
(Brooke Crutchley, University Printer)

Acknowledgements

We are grateful to the following for permission to reprint quotations and illustrations: Ronald Bottrall for *Adam unparadised* (1954); André Deutsch Ltd. for Roy Fuller's *Mythological sonnet xii* from *Brutus's orchard: poems* (1957); Methuen and Company Ltd. for *The world of Paradise Lost*, an engraving by H. F. Hallett, from *Milton's Paradise Lost* edited by G. H. Cowling (1926).

Contents

Square brackets indicate an excerpt from the author or work cited, or analysis of the passage referred to. There is no index.

vii

Preface to the Cambridge Milton

> We have also considered him as a poet, and such he was, if ever human nature could boast it had produced one...in expounding him we have therefore always given, as well as we were enabled, a poetic sense...for a poem, such a one as this especially, is not to be read, and construed, as an Act of Parliament, or a mathematical dissertation; the things of the spirit are spiritually discerned.
>
> JONATHAN RICHARDSON father and son *Explanatory notes and remarks on Paradise Lost* 1734

This volume is part of the Cambridge Milton series. It can be used independently but we assume that you refer as appropriate to two other volumes in particular:

John Milton: introductions A collaborative volume listed under the general editor's name. For Milton's life, times, ideas; music, visual arts, science, the Bible in relation to his poetry; a long essay on *Milton in literary history*; and *General introduction to the early poems.* (Each early poem will also have a specific introduction in its own volume.)

Paradise lost: introduction J. B. Broadbent. General introduction to the poem as a whole with chapters on myth and ritual; epic; history of publication; ideology; structures; allusion; language; syntax; rhetoric; minor components of epic; similes; rhythm; style. This volume also contains a full list of resources (books, art, music etc.); a chronology of the Bible and biblical writings, epics, and other versions of the material of *PL* with cross-references.

Paradise regained and *Samson agonistes* Their volumes will have self-contained introductions.

The series will supersede A. W. Verity's Pitt Press edition of Milton's poetry published from Cambridge 1891 *et seq*. It is designed for use by the individual student, and the class, and the teacher, in schools and colleges, from about the beginning of the sixth form to the end of the BA course in England. Texts are modernized. Notes are on the page they refer to. Introductions and notes aim to provide enough material for the reader to work on for himself, but nothing of a professionally academic kind. Editing is collaborative. We hope that if any volume of text is prescribed for examination, some of its contents will not be set, but left for the student to explore at will.

In the face of the syllabus – heavy for many subjects – 'adventures of ideas' in wider fields, and the time-consuming operations of developing independence of thought...will be undertaken 'at risk'.
> Report of the Welsh Committee of the Schools Council, in Schools Council Working Paper 20, *Sixth form examining methods*, HMSO 1968.

This edition assumes that risk.

Examining, teaching, study

Milton's poems need more annotation to achieve a given degree of comprehension and pleasure than most others. Shakespeare, Donne, Blake, Yeats all demand annotation; but they arouse interest more immediately than Milton does, and so motivate study. This difficulty does not lie in the idleness of the reader or his ignorance: it was felt by Dr Johnson (admittedly a slothful man, but also a learned one and himself an editor). *PL* was one of the first English poems to be annotated. In 1695, twenty-one years after Milton died, Patrick Hume published his *Annotations...Wherein the Texts of Sacred Writ Relating to the Poem, are Quoted; The Parallel Places and Imitations of the Most Excellent Homer and Virgil, Cited and Compared; All the Obscure Parts Render'd in Phrases More Familiar; The Old and Obsolete Words, with Their Originals, Explain'd and Made Easie...* As editors we are all guilty, like Hume, of answering the wrong questions. As examiners, we're guilty of asking them. Milton's poetry is worth using in education because it is difficult; but we have to attend to the right kind of difficulty. In *PL* the serious difficulties are not the surface obscurities of

> nor to which transformd
> *Ammonian Jove*, or *Capitoline* was seen,
> Hee with *Olympias*, this with her who bore
> *Scipio* the highth of *Rome*. IX 507

They are the grave issues of sin, death, 'all our woe', grace, the use of beauty and strength, 'conjugal love'. Those are also the interesting things. But they tend to get left out of editions, and exam papers, because they are more suitable for discussion than for notes and tests. It's the same with Milton's earlier poems. *Arcades* is a little masque he wrote for the Countess of Derby and her family. It has a song that ends

> Though Syrinx your Pan's mistress were,
> Yet Syrinx well might wait on her.
> Such a rural queen
> All Arcadia hath not seen.

In 1969 one of the public examining boards in England asked for 'a brief explanatory note' on those lines. In a way, the answer is simple if indelicate: Pan tried to rape Syrinx so she jumped into a river and turned into a reed. But whatever does it mean in the context? Can the Countess of Derby have suffered such an adventure? Editors are helpless. Verity quotes Tennyson on the preterite subjunctive but does not elucidate; neither, of recent editions, does the most academically distinguished, nor the most school-aimed. I suppose we should be discussing the relationship between goat-god and woman, river and music; that is really difficult.

The best elementary exam on *PL* that I have seen was set in the summer of 1968 on *PL* IV and IX. It asked for either an essay, or a series of shorter answers on a printed passage: so two sorts of candidate were each given a chance to show their best. The essay topic was large yet crucial: in effect, did Adam and Eve *have* to fall? No nonsense about Satan's 'character' dragged in from the Shakespeare paper, or invitations to be romantic about Milton's soul. The printed passage was from Satan's soliloquy on arriving in paradise, and the candidates were told so. Four questions directed the candidate to specific locales – 'What do the phraseology and form of these four lines tell you about Satan's own nature?' for instance. The fifth asked for the passage to be related to its parallel in Book IX. In short, the candidates' memory and attention were being helped; but they were being asked seriously difficult questions.

Here are some suggestions for overcoming the difficulties of Milton's poetry in spite of the editor:

Editing. Never learn footnotes. On the contrary, annotate parts of the text for yourself. You will find the answers to most problems in *Brewer's dictionary of phrase and fable* and the *Shorter Oxford English dictionary*; occasionally you may need a classical dictionary (such as Keats learned out of), a handbook to English and European literature

L i·c· Lempriere

(e.g. the Penguin *Companions to literature*), and a concordance to the Bible.

Performance. Study Milton's poetry out loud to elicit its variousness:

And cast the dark foundations deep	*Nativity* 123
Trip the pert fairies and the dapper elves	*Comus* 118
When that comes think not thou to find me slack	*PR* III 398

To study aloud means reading aloud to understand: alone and together; against music, setting to music, chanting if you like. It includes acting the poetry. Don't try to act, say, the Muses and Old Camus in *Lycidas*; but express in a physical way (especially passively) some of the qualities or states of existence that occur in the poem: e.g. look for the words applied to Lycidas's corpse (float, welter, hurled) and enact them.

Performance may include other kinds of manipulation. Consider how much we use other poetry – hymns, liturgy, pop songs, metaphors, riddles, ritualistic puns and fantasies. Extend the material from 'poetry' to include the sort of thing that Milton's poetry contains – language, mythology, theology, geography – and it becomes clear that we could *use* Milton's poetry in all sorts of ways, if we were not afraid. The advantage of great poetry is that you can criticize it: it stands up to you, and so gives you an idea, gradually, of what is durable and what disposable, or likely to rot. But another advantage of great poetry is that you can do many things with it. Other poets are not afraid to manipulate:

The sun and the moon shall be dark, and the stars shall withdraw their shining. *Joel* ii 10

O dark, dark, dark, amid the blaze of noon,
Irrecoverably dark, total eclipse
Without all hope of day! *Samson* 80

O dark dark dark. They all go into the dark,
The vacant interstellar spaces, the vacant into the vacant,
T. S. ELIOT *East Coker*

There Milton manipulates the Bible, Eliot manipulates Milton. We could probably enrich our own experience of the *Samson* passage better than this through music or paint – as Handel and Rembrandt did. Try representing in a non-verbal medium a sun which is as silent as an invisible moon.

4

Analysis. As you perform and manipulate the work, much of what it is about will emerge. Now start to analyse it more consciously. The best way to do this at first is on the fairly large scale of shape and structure. ✓

What is the shape of this poem? How do its ups and downs go? Where are the soft pastoral parts, and where the strident military ones? If I shut my eyes and transform my image of the poem into colours, or music, a journey, a body, a life, what is it like? I notice in the middle of *Lycidas* a knot of darkness, clanging metal, infection, greed, blows. Can I refine my account, arrange it in terms of a single metaphor? What are those things doing in the poem anyway? How do they relate to the flatness at the very end, the spread out hills, the distant sea, the set sun?

Then, what features in the poem set up structures of their own? This often happens with items that are repeated. The sun in *Lycidas* recurs, along with other stars, with planets, with the moon, and with concepts of the year, time, ripeness and so on; it seems to oppose the weltering waves.

Comprehension. Before interpreting *Lycidas*, though, we have to check our comprehension of its details: e.g. why does Phoebus in line 77 rank as part of the star structure? I put it this late in the process because most of our small-scale difficulties will be solved as we perform and analyse the poetry. To put it in editorial terms, an inch of introduction is worth a yard of footnote.

Examiners have a fondness for those parts of Milton's work which (like the arguments in Pandemonium) have a paraphrasable content. Unfortunately, Milton is practically unparaphrasable, especially in such contexts. His language contains little in the way of metaphors to *cf. Ricks* be unpacked. It is impregnable, for it works in large blocks of idiosyncratic syntax. Soon after you start to analyse the argument you find you have forgotten where it began. Milton's poetry does need a special kind of comprehension; but it is to be tested not by trying to 'translate' or 'construe' Milton; but by acquiring a sense of what you need to know. When you have grasped, by performance, and by structural analysis, what a poem or passage is about, look closely at the words which don't fit your understanding. In *Lycidas* you don't know where Mona, Bellerus and Namancos are. Look them up and you will find they are Anglesey, Land's End and so on. But these identities don't matter. What matters is, first, that Milton should have clad them in old names and mythology; and, second, that they are all western; they ring the sea where Lycidas drowned, and ring the sunset. In short, it is more important to register quality than learn genealogy.

How, though, can you recognize your need for knowledge in the case of an isolated word? Quite often, you can't. A lot of our ignorance has to *wait* to be informed, gradually, often accidentally. But you can avoid some traps by, again, attending to the verse and the structure, e.g.:

> Russet lawns and fallows grey
> *L'allegro* 71

The colours enclose the landscape, so obviously they are important. Try to visualize the line and you will at once feel the need for help.

> Peace, brother, be not over-exquisite
> To cast the fashion of uncertain evils.
> *Comus* 359

As often in Shakespeare, you can't put any expression into the lines until you have found out what the words mean.

Attention

The reader of Milton must be always up on duty: he is surrounded with sense, it rises in every line, every word is to the purpose; there are no lazy intervals, all has been considered, and demands, and merits observation. Even in the best writers you sometimes find words and sentences which hang on so loosely you may blow 'em off; Milton's are all substance and weight. If this be called obscurity, let it be remembered that it is such an obscurity as is a compliment to the reader; not that vicious obscurity which proceeds from a muddled head.

Coleridge copied that into his commonplace book out of the *Explanatory notes on PL* of 1734 by Jonathan Richardson, the painter, and his son. Consider what the parallel in your ordinary life might be of the kind of attention you could give to Milton.

This edition of Milton

The texts are based on the latest editions published in his lifetime: i.e. chiefly *Poems of Mr John Milton, both English and Latin* (the earlier poems) 1645; and the second edition of *PL* 1674. But the text has no authority as such.

The spelling has been modernized (except where it would completely alter pronunciation, e.g. *anow* has been changed to *enow* but not to *enough*).

Stress marks (') have been added where Milton seems to have intended a stress unusual for us, e.g. *óbscene*. Grave accents (`) have been added to indicate voiced syllables in such cases as *blessèd* and in unfamiliar names, e.g. *Atè*. Milton distinguished between stressed and unstressed forms of *hee, he, their, thir*, etc. These have all been reduced to their normal modern forms.

Milton showed much elision of *e*'s, e.g. 'th'obscene dread of Moab's sons', 'th'heav'ns'. These have been omitted too because the elision comes more naturally if we read it with our usual neutral *e* sounds in such cases, than if we try to say *thóbscene* or *theavns*.

On the other hand, Milton's punctuation has been left almost untouched. It is not the same as ours, but you soon get used to it, and to tamper would alter the rhythm. In particular, modern punctuation would interrupt the flow of ideas. For example, a passage about Eve's hair:

> She as a veil down to the slender waist
> Her unadornèd golden tresses wore
> Dishevelled, but in wanton ringlets waved
> As the vine curls her tendrils, which implied
> Subjection, but required with gentle sway,
> And by her yielded, by him best received,
> Yielded with coy submission, modest pride,
> And sweet reluctant amorous delay.   *PL* IV 304

Pause at each punctuation mark. Pause at all awkward line-changes, e.g. 'implied / Subjection' puts a pause equal to a whole stress between the lines. Let all neutral vowels stay neutral, e.g. *tendrils, required, yielded*. Run over unstressed words as in ordinary speech, e.g. 'She as a veil' is nearly as elided as 'She's a veil'; but give all stressed syllables their full value. Don't be officious with the syntax; its sense is impressionistic rather than logical. The words implied–required–yielded–received are set in a pattern which represents a relationship, not a grammar; Eve's hair implies subjection; Adam requires that subjection of her, gently; she does actually yield – also perhaps gently; and he receives it, takes it back again – and then she goes on yielding it, her yielding and her reluctance to yield both an expression of love, her *delay* the rhyming answer to his *sway* (= power). It is not a sentence but a dance. Milton's meanings are often etymological, e.g. *dishevelled* does not mean unkempt but let down without coiffure; *reluctant* does not mean unwilling but resistant; these meanings will emerge more easily if the words are dwelt on and given their full syllabic value – *dis-chevelled, re-luctant*. Reading Hopkins helps because he uses words etymologically. But do not

7

elocute. Actors' voices have a particularly bad effect on Milton because his language is hardly ever beautiful or emotive – it is stiff and thoughtful, or colloquial and definite:

> The leaf was darkish, and had prickles on it,
> But in another country, as he said,
> Bore a bright golden flower, but not in this soil.   *Comus* 631

>   but all sat mute,
> Pondering the danger with deep thoughts; and each
> In other's countenance read his own dismay
> Astonished.   *PL* II 420

In the second passage there, one might emphasize the emotions of dismay and astonishment; but as a matter of fact, *astonished* means *dismayed*; and what matters is the shape, the structure of the lines; it is that, not expressiveness, which represents the fallen angels' bafflement. The structure runs: an angel – another angel – own dismay – more dismay. It is better to read with an eye to semantics than to histrionics; and to read as Milton did (with a provincial accent, rather harshly, with something of a sarcastic note, rolling his *r*'s) than with elegance.

Paradise Lost: Introduction

Myth and ritual

Prometheus and Pandora

ROY FULLER *Mythological sonnet xii*

> That the dread happenings of myth reveal
> Our minds' disorder is a commonplace.
> Myths, too, are history's forgotten face
> Remoulded by desire, though we will feel
> Compared with myths contemporary life unreal.
> Tower and wall may sink without a trace
> But the strong sense of lust and of disgrace
> Lives on.
>   Ourselves have seen Prometheus steal
> The fire the overlords denied to man,
> Which act enchained him to Caucasian rocks.
> We still await the hero that must free
> The great conception whose ambiguous plan
> At once brought to the world its evil box
> And the sole chance to share felicity.
>
>   *Brutus's orchard: poems* 1957

Paradise lost IV 705–19

>   Here in close recess
> With flowers, garlands, and sweet-smelling herbs
> Espousèd Eve decked first her nuptial bed,
> And heavenly choirs the hymenean sung,
> What day the genial angel to our sire
> Brought her in naked beauty more adorned,
> More lovely than Pandora, whom the gods
> Endowed with all their gifts, and O too like
> In sad event, when to the unwiser son
> Of Japhet brought by Hermes, she ensnared
> Mankind with her fair looks, to be avenged
> On him who had stole Jove's authentic fire.

I introduce parts of *Paradise lost* with signposts, or raw material,
rather than map or finished product. It is central to this chapter to
consider how these excerpts use Prometheus, and whether Milton's
sin is equivalent to our disgrace for the bomb. You may, though,
prefer to move on to another set of materials first.

Mythic outline of PL with some analogues

I, VI

ANGELS REBEL AGAINST GOD   SON DEFEATS THEM   THEY FALL TO
HELL
   Babylonian myth: Marduk defeats Tiamat the monster of chaos.

   Greek myth: Uranus the sky-god imprisons his children the Cyclopes in Tartarus; his son Cronos castrates and dethrones him; but Cronos also fetters the Cyclopes, and the Giants and other monsters; and swallows his own children. One of his children, Zeus, is saved, releases the prisoners and dethrones Cronos; but in his turn shuts up the Titans in Tartarus.
   Mythically, defeat of rebels = defeat of chaos = creation of order and establishment of a productive enclave (garden, marriage; parodied by the fallen angels' civilizing of hell in II).

II, VII

SATAN'S VOYAGE THROUGH CHAOS TO EDEN
   SON'S CREATION OF WORLD OUT OF CHAOS
   Babylonian myth: Marduk makes heaven and earth out of the two halves of Tiamat.
   Greek myth: see various accounts in Graves' *Greek myths*.

IV–V, VII–VIII

ADAM AND EVE IN GARDEN OF EDEN AND ACCOUNTS OF THEIR
CREATION
   Greek mythology: Prometheus made man out of his tears and clay.
   Mythically, the original 'garden' is historical both for the race (start of cultivation but not yet of cities) and the individual (garden of childhood).

IX

FALL OF ADAM AND EVE
   Sumerian mythology: Enki cursed for eating sacred plant.
   Norse mythology: serpent at root of the world ashtree Yggdrasil.
   Greek mythology: Prometheus steals fire from the gods and gives it to man.
   Many other myths of a fall from primal simplicity. The crux is always a change in way of life. This may cause disaster (the evils of Pandora's box, and Deucalion's flood, were punishments for the stolen fire); or be the result of disaster (many myths start with a flood or other cataclysm of which the survivors are effectively the first men).

X–XII

SHAME   CARNIVORES   BAD WEATHER   FLOOD   HISTORY   OF   WORLD
EXPULSION
   Nearly all mythologies have a flood. It may be seen as a reflux to the watery chaos, requiring a new start. The expulsion is mythically unusual: it is characteristic of Christianity to see myth running into history, and history into eternity, at both ends.

Middle-eastern myths behind Genesis

Sumerian paradise myth

Engraved on a tablet at Nippur about the 18th century BC but composed much earlier. (The tablet found *c.* 1900; see S. N. Kramer ed. *Enki and Ninhursag: a Sumerian 'paradise' myth* New Haven 1945.) There is a place like the garden of Eden. The hero Enki is put under a curse for eating certain plants. He is attended by a healing goddess called Nin-ti. Nin-ti means both 'lady of the rib' and 'lady who makes live'. In Hebrew, Eve is Hawwah = she who makes live.

Babylonian creation myth

Engraved on seven tablets for the library of Assur-bani-pal in the 7th century BC but composed much earlier. (The Hebrews were in captivity in Babylon in the 6th and 5th centuries BC.) The supreme god 'glorifies' his son Marduk. Marduk fights on the side of order and light against Tiamat and defeats her. Tiamat is a female dragon or snake, goddess of the salt chaos; her forces include a host of devils and monsters. Marduk kills her by blowing into her mouth and putting an arrow into her underparts. Then he cuts her in two and of her two vast halves makes heaven and earth.

This myth contributed to the calming of chaos in *Genesis* i; the hints of a war in heaven; various Tiamat-like creatures including the serpent, leviathan, the Whore of Babylon. The Babylonian and Hebrew creation myths were probably associated with New Year rituals which included a token struggle between the delivering god and monster of the chaotic waters.

There are faint recollections in the Bible of a female consort for Jahweh, called Anath; but she has been lost to Christianity and replaced by the Virgin Mary. In *PL* the Virgin is lost and replaced by Sin. Milton's Sin is much more like the original Tiamat – snaky, an inhabitant of chaos, spawner of the monster Death, and sexually related to Satan. In *PL* it is Satan who first conquers chaos – by travelling through it. This is normally the office of the hero or demiurge in myth.

Babylonian epic of Gilgamesh

Less relevant but includes an episode in which the hero Gilgamesh brings the plant of immortality from the depths of the sea and has it stolen by the serpent. There is also a primitive man called Enkidu or Eabani.

Biblical sources for war in heaven, fall of rebel angels, hell

There is little about this in the canonical Bible. Angel meant messenger (evangelist). An evil angel was a messenger of ill tidings. Satan meant accuser, remembrancer of evil. The system we know, of Satan as chief of a host of angels evil in themselves, was produced gradually as these materials were used in thinking about the origin of evil. Evil in the sense of nasty was merged with, and then attributed to, evil in the sense of wicked; and the angels who bore evil tidings were made themselves evil. This also shifted the responsibility for evil in the world from God, who is by definition good. You can see similar developments in other areas, e.g. stories of how in barbaric courts the bearers of bad news are executed; the way in which we tend to shift blame from ourselves onto other people (It wasn't me) or onto a split-off part of ourselves designed to be the scapegoat (Something got into me). Another way of getting at the problem is to say, What cause do we propose for what is wrong in the world? Is overpopulation, hunger, war, ugliness, always the result of wickedness? Supposing we accept one of the current theories of the origin of the universe, what happens when we try to attach a moral purpose to it?

Most of the personalizing of Satan and blaming of evil onto him and a host of rebel angels, together with such details as angelic hierarchies, occur as metaphors or allegories, e.g. Isaiah's poem against Babylon:

Thy pomp is brought down to the grave, and the noise of thy viols: the worm is spread under thee, and the worms cover thee. How art thou fallen from heaven, O Lucifer, son of the morning! how art thou cut down to the ground, which didst weaken the nations! For thou hast said in thine heart, I will ascend into heaven, I will exalt my throne above the stars of God: I will sit also upon the mount of the congregation, in the sides of the north: I will ascend above the heights of the clouds; I will be like the most High. Yet thou shalt be brought down to hell... *Isaiah* xiv 11–15

That is quoted in *Luke*: 'And he said unto them, I beheld Satan as lightning fall from heaven' (x 18). Then there is Daniel's vision of when the 'horn made war with the saints' (vii). This in turn was a source for some of the visions in *Revelation*, e.g.

And the fifth angel sounded, and I saw a star fall from heaven unto the earth: and to him was given the key of the bottomless pit. And he opened the bottomless pit; and there arose a smoke out of the pit, as the smoke of a great furnace; and the sun and the air were darkened by reason of

14

the smoke of the pit. And there came out of the smoke locusts upon the earth...And they had a king over them, which is the angel of the bottomless pit, whose name in the Hebrew tongue is Abaddon, but in the Greek tongue hath his name Apollyon. ix

And there appeared another wonder in heaven; and behold a great red dragon, having seven heads and ten horns, and seven crowns upon his heads. And his tail drew the third part of the stars of heaven, and did cast them to the earth...and there was war in heaven: Michael and his angels fought against the dragon; and the dragon fought and his angels, and prevailed not; neither was their place found any more in heaven. And the great dragon was cast out, that old serpent, called the Devil, and Satan, which deceiveth the whole world; he was cast out into the earth, and his angels were cast out with him... xii

This may also be derived from the Babylonian myth about Tiamat, with Michael (the guardian angel of Israel) as Marduk.

Apocrypha and pseudepigrapha

The apocryphal (i.e. of doubtful authority) books of the OT were excluded from Protestant Bibles during the 16th and 17th centuries; but they had elaborated on much of this material, especially angels good and bad, and original sin. The most important for us, though, are *I* and *II Enoch*, sometimes known as *Enoch* and *The book of the secrets of Enoch*. These were rejected by the Jews as well as, later, by the Christians as uncanonical. They are not included even in the apocrypha but are called 'pseudepigrapha'. *I Enoch* was a Hebrew book of the 2nd and 1st centuries BC which survived only in an Ethiopic translation – and even that was lost to the western world until a copy was found in Abyssinia in 1773. However, between about 100 BC and 300 AD it influenced Jewish thought, including the authors of the NT. Its effect was specially strong in doctrines of the Messiah (the title Son of Man occurs first in *Enoch*), hell, devils and resurrection. *II Enoch* had a similar history. It is concerned specially with the creation. As it was written by a Hellenistic Jew living in Egypt, *II Enoch* should be compared with Plato's creation myth in his *Timaeus*. Here is an extract from *I Enoch*:

And I looked and turned to another part of the earth and saw there a deep valley with burning fire. And they brought the kings and the mighty, and began to cast them into this deep valley. And there mine eyes saw how they made their instruments, iron chains of immeasurable weight. And I asked the angel of peace who went with me, saying: 'For whom are these chains being prepared?' And he said unto me: 'These are being prepared for the hosts of Azazel, so that they may take them and cast them into the abyss of complete condemnation, and they shall cover their jaws with rough stones as the Lord of Spirits commanded. And Michael, and Gabriel, and Raphael, and Phanuel shall take hold of them on that great day, and cast them on that day into the burning furnace, that the Lord of Spirits may take vengeance on them for their unrighteousness in becoming subject to Satan and leading astray those who dwell on the earth.' liii–liv

(Phanuel does not appear in *PL* but Gabriel guards paradise in IV, Raphael instructs Adam in V-VIII and Michael instructs him in XI-XII. Azazel appears briefly in I.)

Targums

Some of the Biblical authorities were elaborated by the Targums and the Talmud.

The Targums were Aramaic paraphrases and helpful explanations of the OT for Jewish readers who could no longer read Hebrew, dating from about the 1st century AD. It was in the Targums, e.g., that the serpent of *Genesis* ii is first treated explicitly as Satan.

Hexaëmera

Writings about the six days of creation (Greek $6 + hemera$ = day; now also hexáemeron or hexámeron). The main post-Biblical elaboration, all designed to discuss Christian myth and doctrine in the light of whatever secular philosophy prevailed at the time of writing. Started with St Basil's *Hexameron* in the 4th century AD; flourished till the 8th century, in Greek and Latin; many lost, and none read in the Middle Ages; rediscovered in 16th century when a knowledge of Greek was regained in the west; and were then treated as classical literature. For us the important points are (a) that the hexaëmera actually *were* embodiments of Christian material in a classical language, form and culture; (b) that they tended to rationalize the myth: the six days are as much about cosmology and anthropology as about sin.

We go on now with the sources of other contents of *PL*; but all were influenced by the writings we have just been noting – apocrypha and pseudepigrapha, Talmud and Targums, hexaëmera – as well as by the Bible, and classical mythology.

Myths of creation

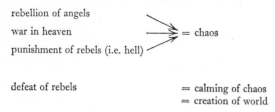

rebellion of angels
war in heaven   = chaos
punishment of rebels (i.e. hell)

defeat of rebels   = calming of chaos
                                    = creation of world

You will find that Milton's imagery tends to confirm these equiva-
lences. E.g. the Son uses the same chariot for calming chaos as for
defeating the rebels; and the incidents are adjacent. This kind of
repetition is frequent in mythology; indeed, it may be essential to
taking a religious world-view. In *The sacred and the profane* Eliade
notes that the initial world is a sacred space. There has to be such a
discontinuity for God to manifest himself in (and for time to begin
in). God makes it by scooping an area out of formlessness and time-
lessness – chaos; but chaos is represented mythically as a shapeless
dragon, a monster of the deep (he really *is* the deep; but we see him
as living *in* it). So defeat of the dragon = creation of the world. To
put it the other way round, we can't think of the world as shaped
without postulating the non-shape of chaos. So far as *PL* is concerned
– or rather, so far as Christianity is concerned – it produces, in the
more rational air, something of a vacuum of significance for one
element or another. You may feel, for instance, that the very elaborate
day-by-day and kind-by-kind account of creation doesn't get us any
further than the initial calming of chaos. You may wonder why the
fall of Satan is described several times over in Books I (by Milton,
Satan and Beelzebub), II (by the peers in Pandemonium, by Sin, and
by Chaos) and III (by Uriel). Of course some of these elements have
a psychological value: the war and fall of the rebels allows for the
exercise of aggression which otherwise tends to be repressed in
Christianity, or turned inwards into self-sacrifice, abstention and
so on.

Genesis ii 4–7 is the earliest extant Hebrew account of creation. It
forms part of that section of *Genesis* known as J, the Jahwistic narrative. It dates from before the Babylonian sacking of Jerusalem in
586 BC and the exile of the Jews into Babylonia.

Genesis i–ii 4 was composed after that exile. It belongs to the P for
'priestly' part of *Genesis*.

These narratives share a good deal with other middle-eastern creation myths (e.g. the watery chaos); but certain items are distinctly Hebrew and have become distinctly Christian: God is not a part of matter or the world, but above it and acting on it independently; he is anthropomorphic, not animal. Man is the lord of creation and made in the image of God. Adam translates a word meaning human being, Man, applied as a name. He communicates directly with God, instead of being separated from him by a hierarchy of demons etc. It is a distinctive feature that he has one woman, Eve (the word means she who gives life).

Many mythologies trace the human race back to a first father and mother – 'our grand parents...our two first parents' (*PL* I 29...III 65) – and *then* one more step back to a *non-sexual* origin:

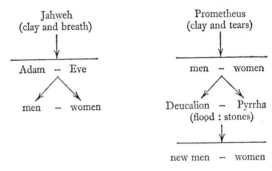

Creation, in other words, is separated from procreation. Does that frontier represent the stage at which men began to understand that children are the result of sexual intercourse? or should we interpret it more psychologically, as the taboo on regarding our parents as sexually active?

The garden of Eden

There is probably a connection between creation and the garden of Eden. The chief text here is an essay by T. H. Robinson in *Myth and ritual of the Hebrews* ed S. H. Hooke (Oxford 1933). Robinson makes a conjectural reconstruction of a pre-exilic fertility ritual.

Both the Babylonians and the Hebrews specialized in New Year festivals. At an early stage, one of these festivals probably took the form of the figures or representatives of Jahweh and his wife Anath being removed from the temple and put in a hut, booth or bower of greenery in the temple courtyard; or perhaps in a vineyard nearby. The story of the battle against the monster of the chaotic waters would be enacted, followed by the marriage of Jahweh and Anath; then the death of Jahweh, and his resurrection; and then the return with Anath to the temple. It seems possible that in this celebration of the recurring seasons, the control of water, the fertilization of crops and so on, we have an origin for paradise; Adam and Eve are then actual god and goddess. Those are conjectural rites, but the Feast of Tabernacles was an actual wine harvest festival, at the Jewish New Year. The people lived in booths of greenery to celebrate it. This is said to have been a form of camping when they came to Jerusalem from distant villages; but it may have been a relic of the older 'groves' in which local gods were worshipped; or of the ritual described above.

Adam and Eve

The authorities are the same as for the elements discussed above. The Biblical account is all contained in *Genesis* i-iii. Creation and fall seem to have little to do with each other mythically; but there is a metaphorical passage in *Ezekiel* where the king of Tyre is likened to the original inhabitant of Eden; in this case it is not Adam but a cherub – in effect Satan. This is a recollection of another version of the myth but it contributed to debates about whether Adam was really human or divine:

Son of man, take up a lamentation upon the king of Tyrus, and say unto him, Thus saith the Lord God; Thou sealest up the sum, full of wisdom, and perfect in beauty. Thou hast been in Eden the garden of God...thou wast upon the holy mountain of God; thou hast walked up and down in the midst of the stones of fire. Thou wast perfect in thy ways from the day that thou wast created, till iniquity was found in thee...Thine heart was lifted up because of thy beauty, thou hast corrupted thy wisdom by reason of thy brightness: I will cast thee to the ground...I made the nations to shake at the sound of his fall, when I cast him down to hell with them that descend into the pit...   *Ezekiel* xxviii...xxxi

You can see from this passage how easily an expression of feeling can be turned, as time goes by, into a statement of history, and so into the basis of doctrine: in this case, hatred of the neighbouring kingdom → description of Adam → original sin.

Temptation and fall

Elaborations of the *Genesis* story in the hexaëmeral books and in textbooks of theology were concerned especially with the sort of questions we naturally ask when myth is presented to us as history: What exactly was the status of Adam and Eve before the fall? At what point did they actually fall? What was the fruit – fig? apple? Much anxiety attached to unfallen sex. If sexual activity is profane (and Ambrose, one of the first hexaëmeral writers, was a proponent of virginity as a holy state), then how could Adam and Eve engage in it before the fall? By some kind of long-range, non-touching method, Augustine suggested. Other elaborations treated the whole story in a 'romantic' way, parallel to the romantic elaborations of epic. *The cave of treasures* is a Syriac prose account dating from the 6th century AD. The cave, stocked with gold, frankincense and myrrh brought from the garden of Eden, is where Adam and Eve first make love, and where Adam is buried. In the Ethiopic *Book of Adam and Eve* of about the same date, Noah saves these treasures from the flood; later the Magi present them to the newborn Christ. The *Cursor mundi* (world history) written in Northumbria in the 14th century has an incident where Seth revisits paradise and finds there a tree with bare branches; its branches reach the sky and its roots reach hell. Round it an adder is coiled and in its upper branches lies a newborn baby.

Eden as a sexual paradise, like the Moslem heaven; the garden of Eden as a garden of love (see Blake's poem of that name, and *The romance of the rose*) – these can make us feel all the more that what happened there was innocent, or was guilty, but either way has little to do with all the other parts of the plot of *PL*. You can see it being put to this use in the last stanza of *Eden* by Hilary Corke:

> Four waters out of Eden flow
> Whose crystal is most cardinal:
> Four angels stand upon the wall.
> Within the wall two lovers stand
> Beneath the passion-fruited bough,
> Are hand in hand, are I and Thou.
> The angels nod with kindly faces:
> All songs are silent now.

See the rest of the poem (in his volume *The early drowned* 1961) for other symbolic uses of that part of the myth.

Anthropology

What actually is the myth about? What is the snake, the tree, the sin? We don't know. The best we can do is consult a dictionary of folklore for elements of the myth such as snake and tree; and read Claude Lévi-Strauss *Mythologiques: le cru et le cuit* (Paris 1964) translated as *The raw and the cooked* (London 1970), with a view to imitating the 'structuralist' methods he uses, which are for the time being the most fruitful. An example of a structure which is partly in this myth and partly out of it may be sketched in this way:

Greek mythology

Zeus king of the gods	gives birth to	the fullgrown goddess Athene out of his head

Milton's invention

Satan king of demons	gives birth to	the fullgrown witch Sin out of his head

Judeo-Christian mythology

The Lord God	creates	the fullgrown man Adam in his own image
The king of creation Adam	gives birth to	his fullgrown queen Eve out of his side

Why is this pattern or structure used?

That such structures exist was recognized very early on, when Christian theologians began to draw parallels between Old Testament items which they saw as 'types' of New Testament ones: Adam's side was opened to produce Eve, Christ's side was opened to produce salvation. This is known as typology.

If we look at the elements snake–tree–woman–sex–fate we shall find many parallels in the mythology of still-primitive cultures. For example (translating Lévi-Strauss's versions):

Mundurucu: the serpent's wife

A woman had a serpent for lover. Under the pretext of collecting fruit she took herself every day into the forest to meet the serpent, who lived in a particular tree. They would make love until evening and, when the moment came to leave, the serpent would shake down enough fruit for the woman to fill her basket. The woman became pregnant; her brother, suspicious, spied on her. Without seeing her lover, he heard her cry in the middle of their lovemaking, 'Don't make me laugh so much, Tupasherébé! You're making me wet myself!' Eventually the brother saw the serpent and killed it...Later, the son that the woman had by the serpent avenged his father.

Tenetehara: sex and punishment

The first man, created by the demiurge, lived in innocence although he possessed a penis constantly erect, whose detumescence he tried vainly to provoke by sprinkling it with manioc soup. Instructed by a water spirit, the first woman taught him how to soften his penis by having an orgasm in intercourse. When the demiurge saw the flaccid penis he was angry and said: From now on you will have a soft penis, you will beget children, and then you will die; your child will grow up, he also will beget a child, and he will die in his turn.

British Guiana: tree and flood

Duid, the creator's brother, fed men with the fruit of the tree of life, but they discovered where he got his supplies from and resolved to provide for themselves. Infuriated by this insubordination, the creator felled the tree, and a flood spurted from its stump.

We may speculate from here along several lines. Lévi-Strauss is directing himself to the shift from raw to cooked food, and other changes associated with it – the change from fungus (i.e. rotten) to fresh vegetables; the need for fire to cook with; the need for fuel for the fire (but at the same time the need to preserve cultivated trees from fire); the need to keep the secret of the cultivated tree (maize, for instance) or you will have to share its fruit with others; problems of irrigation and flooding – fire and water are beneficial as the instruments of cooking, but in other aspects they are dangerous.

There are hints of this in *Genesis*: iii 17–19 is about cultivation, fire and technology come in iv, the flood in vii. These hints are taken up in *PL* x and xi, especially x 1070 about the invention of firemaking. For more on the guiltiness of fire see the myth of Prometheus, which Milton refers to at iv 719.

The myth's bones have been overlaid by millenia of rationalizing. Fire and flood are removed to a later part of the story, and given separate causes. In many myths, the secret of cultivation is let out – often to a woman – by a snake or other animal. He may subvert the creator's purpose; but he is not man's enemy: he is 'the trickster', the joker of the universe, the sly one with secret know-how. In *Genesis*, the trickster's cunning is still there in the snake; but in later interpretations it becomes the subtle evil of the devil inside the snake.

Most paintings of the temptation emphasize its erotic qualities. Raphael's snake bears Eve's head (a frequent motif; sometimes the head is angelic; it is rarely a snake's); and the tree it twists round is phallic. In Michelangelo's painting, Eve's head as she takes the apple lies between Adam's thighs; Titian's Adam touches Eve's breast at the same moment; Tintoretto's Eve, as she offers the apple to Adam, gazes on his genitals. What might the place of the erotic in some earlier stage of the myth then have been? What have snakes to do with sex? And what has sex to do with trees, cultivation, irrigation, fire, cooking, technological secrets?

22

Psychology

Structuralist anthropology takes us in the direction of invention and its anxieties. Psychoanalytic theory takes us towards anxiety about relationships, especially incest. The text here is Freud's *Totem and taboo*. A totem is a thing (usually an animal or plant of some kind) which stands for the tribe or family, like a regimental mascot. Originally the totem was thought of as the ancestor of the family; and perhaps (before people understood that children were the result of coitus) the totem was thought of as the impregnator of the mother. So for people of the same totem to marry would be incest; and to eat or kill your totem would be murder of your relative. So the totem is taboo. You must not harm it; if it is a tree you must not cut it down or eat its fruit or sit in its shade.

Freud's point is that these taboos are relics of an original taboo on incest. He says the prohibition of incest is difficult to explain. It is very ancient so it cannot be based on eugenics – the people of that time would not know about its effect on breeding. It cannot be explained by instinctive aversion because then it would not be necessary to put such a strict prohibition on it. At this stage in his argument, Freud implies that to forbid something is to acknowledge that it is strongly desired. In Christian doctrine, however, the taboo on the tree of knowledge has been rationalized into a test of pure obedience. (You can enact this argument: paint a picture of two trees: one tree that you want very much to eat the fruit of because it is so luscious and desirable; the other that you are interested in only because you have been told not to be. How do the painted trees compare?)

In Freud's mythology, the taboo on incest goes back to 'the primal horde' of early men, and forward to sacred meal or sacrament:

Thus we have the clan, which on a solemn occasion kills its totem in a cruel manner and eats it raw, blood, flesh, and bones. At the same time, the members of the clan, disguised in imitation of the totem, mimic it in sound and movement as if they wanted to emphasize their common identity. There is also the conscious realisation that an action is being carried out which is forbidden to each individual and which can only be justified through the participation of all, so that no one is allowed to exclude himself from the killing and the feast. After the act is accomplished the murdered animal is bewailed and lamented...But after this mourning there follows loud festival gaiety accompanied by the unchaining of every impulse and the permission of every gratification.

Freud goes on to interpret the feast in terms of the yet more primitive experience:

The Darwinian conception of the primal horde does not, of course, allow for the beginning of totemism. There is only a violent, jealous father who keeps all the females for himself and drives away the growing sons.

By basing our argument upon the celebration of the totem we are in a position to give an answer: 'One day the expelled brothers joined forces, slew and ate the father, and thus put an end to the father horde. Together they dared and accomplished what would have remained impossible for them singly. Perhaps some advance in culture, like the use of a new weapon, had given them the feeling of superiority...' The totem feast, which is perhaps mankind's first celebration, would be the repetition and commemoration of this memorable, criminal act with which so many things began, social organisation, moral restrictions and religion.

Freud's myth is also an account of guilt; but the guilt that he deals in differs from the official guilt of Christianity and *PL*. For Freud, guilt is essentially ambivalent. 'They hated the father who stood so powerfully in the way of their sexual demands and their desire for power, but they also loved and admired him.' It is from this ambivalence that guilt and anxiety spring, as they spring in children and in neurosis. The sons in Freud's clan 'undid their deed by declaring that the killing of the father substitute, the totem, was not allowed'; later still, the idea was conceived of a supreme god and it was held to be the god who demanded the festival sacrifice.

Guilt is the expression of the conflict of ambivalence, the eternal struggle between Eros and the destructive or death instinct.

FREUD *Civilisation and its discontents* 1939

In *Life against death: the psychoanalytical meaning of history* Norman O. Brown argues against Freud that the primal crime was not an historical event; yet

It still remains true that each one of us is suffering from the trauma of becoming human, a trauma first enacted in the Ice Age and re-enacted in every individual born in the human family. But the legacy of the trauma is not an objective burden of guilt transmitted by an objective inheritance of acquired characteristics – as Freud postulated – and imposing repression of the organism from outside and from the past, but a fantasy of guilt perpetually reproduced by the ego so that the organism can repress itself.

(VINTAGE ed p. 167)

For the time being we can only select among these materials those which make the most sense, or feel most valid, for us. This cannot be done by ratiocination, or even by deliberate belief. Let your mind dwell on the myth until only its enduring elements remain. There was a change; it is represented in *Genesis* and *PL* by changes in length of life, in weather, abode, sexual habits. There was guilt. There was a

movement outwards, from the safe forested garden to the wilderness
that had to be cultivated. There were grief and pain. These developments are tied back in the mythology to a forbidden tree and a cunning snake. The central change occurs in a garden which does not have
to be cultivated; it is lost for a wilderness which does have to be. In
the garden there are no children; but after the change, outside, there
are not only children but all people, and history.

Here are parts of Ronald Bottrall's *Adam unparadised*; the whole
poem, in his 1954 volume of that title, should be studied as an
interpretation of the myth:

> I have disappointed you, father.
> Those morsels of me that are you, the divine
> Chromosomes, have been crossed with a line
> Of waywardness and a wild feather
> Disfigures my angelic plumage,
> Leaving all heaven in a rage.
> But the tempter spoke so well
> Your still small voice was so distant
> And the fruit so knowledgeable
> That my credulous hand curled like a plant
> Around the obliging apple.

> The animals I pampered and named
> Are roaring within me unashamed;
> Lion, tiger, lynx, the saliva
> Dripping from their jaws. Like Godiva
> I try to cover my nakedness
> From the peeping Toms by a discreet use
> Of natural camouflage, but God's eye
> Is all-seeing and Eve
> Has developed a new curiosity.
> My heart is still on my sleeve...

Ritual

Another way into the myth is ritual. Ritual may have come first anyway:

Ritual is, as it were, the DNA of society, the encoded informational basis
of culture; it is the memory core of human achievement. Myth is the verbal
derivative of ritual, and, with the evolution of writing, the informational
content of ritual has to some extent taken a verbal form. The written early
Sumerian myths are probably only the verbal part of a ritual.
    BERNARD G. CAMPBELL *Human evolution: an introduction to man's adapt-
    ations* 1967 ch. 10

Every myth has a ritual associated with it: crucifixion and eucharist,
exodus and passover, the divine right of kings and coronation. We are

not sure which came first; and in any case behind them both must lie ordinary experience.

Consider what experiences *might* lie behind Little Red Riding Hood; what ritual and myth *might* embody it; and what doctrines *might* be built on it.

Little Red Riding Hood

1 Observation of simple facts: there are green woods, with flowers and wolves in them; young girls in red clothes; old women.

2 Anxiety about survival: in the wood you can be lost, afraid, hungry. The wolf can eat you. A hungry man might – no. Old women cannot feed themselves: they die.

3 More sophisticated anxieties: animism, taboo, religion. Is the wood haunted (with the ghosts of unfed grannies?). Perhaps the flowers belong to the ghosts, or are the ghosts: don't pick them. The wolf may be treated animistically, as if it were a person; so now its dangerousness becomes malice, it is a conscious enemy of mankind. If we let granny die perhaps the whole tribe will die: her bed is the tribe's womb. Granny has now become a goddess; and so far as the wolf represents death he is her (i.e. the tribe's) enemy; and the god of death, the grave, underworld, hell.

4 Ritual (assuming it comes before myth): we will send a girl through the wood for the wolf to eat, to appease him. Or, we will send a girl through the wood to give granny fertility again (a kiss, flowers, food) that the tribe may live for ever. At first, this would actually happen; then it would become a play, a ritual.

5 A myth that tells the story of the ritual. Already it contains many of the structural conventions of epic: a perilous journey, partly through a dark and dangerous wood (descent to the underworld) where the hero/ine picks taboo flowers (Persephone, Eve, golden bough of *Aeneid* VI); pastoral scene; return, fight etc.

6 Romance: there are in fact a number of different versions of the folktale of Little Red Riding Hood and for our purposes we can regard these as parallels to the romanticization of epic in the 16th century. In the most romantic versions, the girl meets a party of woodcutters on her way through the wood; one of them follows her; she finds the wolf disguised in granny's nightcap (disguise standard in romance); the woodcutter rushes in, kills the wolf, slits it open and out pops granny none the worse (magical resurrection). A further step makes the woodcutter the lover of Little Red Riding Hood.

7   Etiology: at some stage, the original observations on which all this has been based will become overlaid with more sophisticated assumptions as to what the myth means. Probably the first would be an etiological explanation: i.e. you consider the story and say 'So that's why wolves won't eat widows' or 'why wolves have seams up their bellies'. The myth of *Genesis* ii has often been interpreted etiologically: it 'explains' why we die, have to work, have labour pains, don't like snakes, and why snakes slither.

8   Ethics: now moral lessons will be drawn from the story; some of them will be quite different from the originating anxieties, e.g. Don't talk to strange men (they may be wolves in disguise). It is forbidden to pick the flowers. 'My mother told me I never should...' At a further stage, the story will be elaborated to show that Little Red Riding Hood had sinned, probably by picking the flowers, and therefore deserved more than she got.

9   Theology: at that stage, when sin enters, the heroine comes to stand for sinful mankind, the wolf is Satan or Death, the woodcutter is Christ (harrowing hell, for instance) and the flowers are Forbidden Fruit.

10   Allegory: usually associated with romance and moral interpretation. Clearly, the wood will be seen as life's pilgrim way and, in the manner of allegory, will be filled with significant details: granny's cottage will have symbolic architecture; her nightcap, as worn by the wolf, will become the Head-dress of Duplicity, and so on.

11   Psychoanalytic reinterpretation: granny *is* the wolf and Little Red Riding Hood wants to be eaten/raped by her/him. The woodcutter is also a split-off, 'good' version of the wolf so she gets what she wants anyway. Another version, rather more allegorical: granny/wolf is the family womb; the woodcutter rescues the girl from servitude to it and sets her up as an independent adult.

It sounds funny written out like this; but then so does pantomime, and pantomime appeals because it is deadly serious.

PL as enactment

To grasp the plot of *PL* as myth, turn it into ritual again, by acting one of the mystery plays of creation, fall, flood and so on (they are referred to in the section on epic). You will get even closer, though, if you perform an impromptu mime of the essential story. Attend to the passive sensations.

For example, God the Father: high, immobile, unspeaking, eyes unfocused, 'consulting on the sum of things secure'. The actor tries to guess the sensations of omnipotence, and of being a quite different being from others; of not having been born, for instance. Angels: what is it like to have such natures? What is worship? The Son: what is it like to be the favourite child? and not to be? Rebellion: some angels conspire – the word means breathe together. Other scenes would be easier.

Myth is the mode of simultaneous awareness of a complex group of causes and effects.
Electrical circuitry confers a mythic dimension on our ordinary individual and group actions. Our technology forces us to live mythically, but we continue to think fragmentarily, and on single, separate planes.
Myth means putting on the audience, putting on one's environment.

MARSHALL MCLUHAN and QUENTIN FIORE *The medium is the massage: an inventory of effects* 1967

Epic

Form and hero

Myth can take various forms; so can history. *PL* contains both, in the form of an epic. The renaissance idea of epic was a large narrative poem, with some reference to the gods, and a grand hero. The hero's deeds may be partly historical. They celebrate the nation in which the poem is produced. The hero is often seen as the founder of that nation. (So we may suppose that epic is a nationalistic genre; it is a literary form of ancestor-worship; it will assume respect for time and for authority – be conservative, in fact. Not the most convenient form for a revolutionary like Milton.)

Military epic

The form of epic, and especially its heroes' qualities, change with changes in society. Primitive societies produce epics whose heroes are most active in single combat: the Babylonian Gilgamesh or the Anglo-Saxon Beowulf conquers men and monsters to display the most important virtues of the time – strength, courage, loyalty:

Hwæt! We gar-dena   in geardagum,
þeodcyninga   þrym genfrunon,
hu ða æþelingas   ellen fremedon...

Hi! We have heard of the force of the kings of Danish spears in days past, how the chieftains did great things. Often did Scyld son of Scef beat down hordes of foes from many tribes: he made fear fall upon them. From being found as a baby abandoned his fortunes turned, he grew great under the heavens into high honour, till all who dwell around the whale-stream's shores must obey and yield him tribute. He was a good king.

That is of the Iron Age. The Greek epics *Iliad* and *Odyssey* refer to the Bronze Age, which is technologically more primitive than Iron; and the Greek epics were composed perhaps 1,500 years before the Anglo-Saxon. But as literature, and in some cultural aspects, they are more advanced. They still concentrate on warfare, but it is organized between armies; there may be fights with monsters but there is also intervention by anthropomorphic gods; and as the world is more complicated, so are the heroes – Achilles sulks, Odysseus travels home to a wife threatened by suitors and is tempted on the way by Circe.

Here are the openings of the *Iliad* and the *Odyssey:*

The wrath of Achilles is my theme, that fatal wrath which, in fulfilling the will of Zeus, brought the Achaeans so much suffering and sent the gallant souls of many noblemen to Hades, leaving their bodies as carrion for the dogs and passing birds. Let us begin, goddess of song, with the angry parting that took place between Agamemnon king of men and the great Achilles son of Peleus. Which of the gods was it that made them quarrel?

trans. RIEU 1950

Tell me, Muse,
Of the man of many ways [Odysseus],
Who was driven far journeys,
After he had sacked Troy's sacred citadel.
Many were they whose cities he saw,
Whose minds he learned of,
Many the pains he suffered in his spirit on the wide sea,
Struggling for his own life and the homecoming of his companions.

trans. LATTIMORE 1965

In both those stages, of Greek and Anglo-Saxon, epics were composed orally, and perhaps by more than one author, to be recited to the harp at feasts. It was only later that they were written down. Oral poetry requires repetition, standardized phrases and so on to help memory and audibility; these techniques were carried on into the third, literary stage. Here an individual poet, such as Virgil, living in a much more complicated society, sits down in a city to write an epic celebrating his nation. For Virgil, in Rome about 20 BC, the hero was

Aeneas, the legendary Trojan who escaped from Troy and founded Rome:

Of arms I sing and of the man who first, driven in exile from the coasts of Troy, came to Italy and Lavinian shores. In the end, through much suffering poured on sea and land from Juno's relentless enmity, and through much also that he endured in war, he was to build a city and set up his gods in Latium; whence came the Latin race, the lords of Alba and the walls of lofty Rome. [See Poussin's painting of *Venus bringing arms to Aeneas* – the Rouen version – as a frontispiece for 17c feelings about the *Aeneid*.]

By now the oral techniques have become conventions, conscious effects of style, no longer needed for production but used in order to join the present to the past: Virgil's imitations of Homer are meant to show that Roman civilization is not upstart but the heir of Greek and Trojan culture.

Romantic epic

In the Middle Ages, two new elements entered the epic form: romance and Christianity. Romance here means knight-errantry; romantic love; magic; allegory. The most famous epics of the 16th century are romantic. The society they celebrate is not so much a tribe or even a nation, as Christendom. Ariosto's *Orlando furioso* ('Roland raving' 1532) is about Charlemagne's defence of Christian Europe against the Saracens; but there are several love stories in it and an ascent to the moon on a hippogriff to fetch back Orlando's lost sanity (cf. the Limbo of Fools in *PL* III). Here is the first stanza as translated, on the orders of Queen Elizabeth, by Sir John Harington in 1591:

> Of dames, of knights, of arms, of love's delight,
> Of courtesies, of high attempts, I speak,
> Then when the Moors transported all their might
> On Africk seas, the force of France to break,
> Incited by the youthful heat and spite
> Of Agramont their king, that vowed to wreak
> The death of King Traiano (lately slain)
> Upon the Roman Emperor Charlemagne.

In 1576 another Italian poet, Torquato Tasso, completed *Gerusalemme liberata*. This is an epic on the crusades – the later aggressive stage in that long struggle that Europe made, after the collapse of the Roman Empire, to reassert itself against the races south and east of the Mediterranean. Its hero is the crusader Godfrey of Boulogne who besieges Jerusalem. It was translated under the title *Godfrey of*

Boulogne or Jerusalem delivered by Edward Fairfax in 1600. You can
see from the opening how the chivalric romance is moving towards
the cosmic epic of *Paradise lost*:

> The sacred armies and the godly knight
> That the great sepulchre of Christ did free,
> I sing. Much wrought his valour and foresight
> And in that glorious war much suffered he;
> In vain 'gainst him did Hell oppose her might,
> In vain the Turks and Morians armèd be;
> His soldiers wild (to brawls and mutines pressed)
> Reducèd he to peace, so heaven him blessed.
>
> O heavenly muse, that not with fading bays
> Deckest thy brow by th' Heliconian spring,
> But sittest crowned with stars' immortal rays
> In heaven where legions of bright angels sing,
> Inspire life in my wit, my thoughts upraise,
> My verse ennoble, and forgive the thing
> If fictions light I mix with truth divine
> And fill these lines with others' praise than thine.

God appears as a capricious Jove (1 17, IX 57); Hell is furnished with
gridirons and monsters (IV); the wizard's niece Armida lures knights
to her enchanted gardens:

> There on a table was all dainty food
> That sea, that earth or liquid air could give,
> And in the crystal of the laughing flood
> They saw two naked virgins bathe and dive
> That sometimes toying, sometimes wrastling stood,
> Sometimes for speed and skill in swimming strove,
> Now underneath they dived, now rose above
> And 'ticing baits laid forth of lust and love.   xv 58

The church authorities made Tasso add a key, allegorizing scenes like
this as temptations of the pilgrim soul. In that light they were imitated
by Milton (e.g. *PR* II 337) and Spenser (Bower of Bliss, *FQ* II xii).

Ariosto celebrated the expansionist drive of Europe in terms of
Charlemagne; Tasso in terms of the crusades. It was celebrated more
directly, in terms of the very recent, by the Portugese poet Luis de
Camoens. His epic title *Os Lusiads* means the sons of Lusus, mythical
settler of Lusitania, i.e. Portugal; so his title is really *The Portugese*.
It was published in 1572 but not translated into English until 1655
(by Sir Richard Fanshawe, ambassador to Madrid, as *The Lusiads*).
Camoens's hero is Vasco da Gama, who in 1498 was the first modern
European to sail across the Indian Ocean. As a later translator,
Mickle, said in 1776, the *Lusiads* is the 'epic poem of the birth of

commerce, and, in a particular manner, the epic poem of whatever country has the control and possession of the commerce of India'. In Mickle's day the British were taking over India, so he cut much of Camoens's patriotism out of the poem and inserted his own. The *Lusiads* raises the issue of epic as a form more tightly related than most to society – society on the scale of nation. You might regard it as the expression of aggressive nationalism, or aggressive catholicism; at any rate as a form deriving from incipient capitalism (though you would then have to account for the Homeric epics in, probably, a rather different way). Certainly, more than with most art forms you can say of an epic, 'this poem indicates so-and-so about the culture from which it sprang'.

The more local interest of the *Lusiads* is this: it shows how important the East was to Europe – more important than America, until the 19th century. It was important, obviously, for trade; but also as a source of aesthetic wealth. Milton's most exotic glimpse –

> India and the golden Chersoness,
> And utmost Indian isle Tapróbane,
> Dusk faces with white silken turbants wreathed

PR IV 74

– is drawn from the world of the *Lusiads*. Perhaps people living in small homogeneous countries like England, Holland, Portugal, colonized the world not only for power but also because they needed contact with strangeness, as much anyway as they needed the 'spicy drugs' of Ternate and Tidore (*PL* II 640).

In Ireland, through the 1580s and 90s, Edmund Spenser wrote but never finished his romance *The Fairy Queen*. It is highly patriotic but not colonialist – perhaps because Spenser was himself, in effect, exiled in the smouldering colony of Ireland. Behind the action King Arthur stands as national hero, and Queen Elizabeth as heroine; but they exist more as brooding deities than agents. The ethos is that of Christian humanism, but the knights in the poem direct their energies at perfecting their own behaviour rather than changing other people's. Each book recites the adventures of a knight who represents one virtue; so the work lacks the concentrated heroism of epic. Here are some of the contents:

Book I		Red Cross Knight (George)	Holiness
	Canto v	Hell	
Book II		Sir Guyon	Temperance
	v	Acrasia's bower	
	vi	Phaedria's Isle Idle Lake	

Anti-romance

About 1600 the fashion for heroic romance began to fade. In two parts, 1605 and 1615, Miguel de Cervantes Saavedra produced Spain's great contribution to the European epic, *Don Quixote*. Cervantes had a romantic life himself – wounded in battle, captured by pirates, imprisoned in Algiers; yet in *Don Quixote* he wrote a mock romance. It turned, though, into something more humane than any genuine romance, or than any mock epic such as the *Dunciad*; it turned into a novel starting the line of *Tristram Shandy* and Joyce's *Ulysses*:

At a certain village in La Mancha, of which I cannot remember the name, there lived not long ago one of those old-fashioned gentlemen, who are never without a lance upon a rack, an old target, a lean horse, and a greyhound. His diet consisted more of beef than mutton; and with minced meat on most nights, lentils on Fridays, griefs and groans on Saturdays, and a pigeon extraordinary on Sundays, he consumed three-quarters of his revenue; the rest was laid out in a plush coat, velvet breeches, with slippers of the same, for holidays; and a suit of the very best homespun cloth which he bestowed on himself for working days...You must know, then, that when our gentleman had nothing to do (which was almost all the year round) he passed his time in reading books of knight-errantry, which he did with that application and delight that at last he in a manner wholly left off his country sports, and even the care of his estate; nay, he grew so strangely besotted with these amusements, that he sold many acres of arable land to purchase books of that kind...and thus by sleeping little, and reading much, the moisture of his brain was exhausted to that degree, that at last he lost the use of his reason. A world of disorderly notions, picked out of his books, crowded into his imagination; and now his head was full of nothing but enchantments, quarrels, battles, challenges, wounds, complaints, amours, torments, and abundance of stuff and impossibilities; insomuch, that all the fables and fantastical tales which he read, seemed to him now as true as the most authentic histories.   trans. MOTTEUX 1700

And so Don Quixote turns knight-errant himself. The kind of book Cervantes was mocking was the undergrowth of popular romance, some verse and some prose. The stories had been extant for centuries and spread wider during the 16th century after the invention of printing. They related to, say, *Gerusalemme liberata* rather as pulp science-fiction relates to *Brave new world*. Yet even as late as 1667 there was something to be abjured, for Milton abjured it:

> Not sedulous by nature to indite
> Wars, hitherto the only argument
> Heroic deemed, chief maistrie to dissect
> With long and tedious havoc fabled knights
> In battles feigned (the better fortitude
> Of patience and heroic martyrdom
> Unsung), or to describe races and games,
> Or tilting furniture, emblazoned shields,
> Impresses quaint, caparisons and steeds;
> Bases and tinsel trappings, gorgeous knights
> At joust and tournament; then marshalled feast
> Served up in hall with sewers, and seneschals.   *PL* IX 27

He was more intent on the other new element, Christianity.

Christianity

The fall (bababadalgharaghtakamminarronnkonnbronntonnerronntuonn-thunntrovarrhounawnskawntoohoohoordenenthurnuk!) of a once wallstrait oldparr is retaled early in bed and later on life down through all christian minstrelsy.   JAMES JOYCE *Finnegans wake* 1939

In the epics of Ariosto, Camoens and Tasso, Christianity had been the zeal of colonizing Europeans, merchant missionaries; in Spenser, Christianity was veiled in allegory. Milton wanted to deal not just with Christendom as a realm in space and time, but with Christianity as worldwide and eternal religious truth; he wanted to be explicit; and he wanted to write with a gravity and strictness which he felt to be both more pure, and more classical, than the proliferant incident and decoration of the romantic epics.

The monks of Anglo-Saxon England had done this in their re-tellings of Bible stories in heroic verse, early in the 8th century – poems now referred to as *Genesis*, *Exodus*, *Christ and Satan* and so on. Of these, the two poems dealing with *Genesis* (*Genesis A* and *B*) are the most relevant. They were at one time attributed to Caedmon, the cowherd poet of Whitby monastery. In fact *Genesis B* seems to be a translation from a German poem inserted into the MS; but *Genesis A* probably was composed by a monk of little learning and rather careful Christianity. The religion had been established here for only 100 years or so, and the author, though working from a Latin Bible, was

34

clearly inspired by native epic. We have already referred to *Beowulf* as an example of straight military epic. It was probably put into its final form a few years after these Bible poems; but it stood for a whole body of Anglo-Saxon poetry which was heroic in the original Homeric sense: it told of the actual treks and battles of migrating tribes. Indeed there are monsters, but they seem as real as Red Indians, or the Devil, seem to other heroes. It shows how close they were to the 'original' kind of epic that, in a mystical poem called *The dream of the Rood*, Christ on the cross is described as *hæleþ*, hero.

Milton may have seen some of the Anglo-Saxon Bible poems. The only known MSS were acquired by a man he knew, called Francis Junius in international Latin – François Du Jon, a Dutch printer who came to work in England as a librarian. He was the first great scholar of Germanic culture and could read Old High German and Old Norse as well as Anglo-Saxon. He left this 'Caedmon MS' to the British Museum when he died in 1677. It is illustrated with pictures of the fall of the rebel angels and so on. Here are some extracts as translated by R. K. Gordon (*Anglo-Saxon poetry* Everyman n.d.):

Genesis A

They performed naught in heaven save right and truth, till the leader of the angels in his pride fell into error. They would no longer follow their own way of life, but turned from the love of God. They made great boasting that they could share with God the glorious abode, wide and radiant, amid the splendour of the host. Grief came upon them there, envy and presumption and the pride of that angel who first began to work and weave and stir up that wickedness, when, thirsting for strife, he declared that he would possess a dwelling and throne in the northern part of the kingdom of heaven!...Nothing had then been wrought here as yet save darkness, but this wide land stood, sunk and dark, remote from God, empty and useless. The resolute King looked thereon with his eyes, and beheld the place bare of joys, saw the dark mist brooding in eternal night, black under the heavens, sombre and waste, till at the command of the glorious King this creation came into being...

Genesis B

Satan uttered speech; he who henceforth must needs dwell in hell, have the abyss in his keeping, spoke in sorrow – he was once God's angel, radiant in heaven, until his mind led him astray, and his pride most strongly of all, so that he would not honour the word of the Lord of hosts. Within him pride swelled about his heart, outside him was hot grievous torment. He spoke these words.

'This desolate place is very different from that other which once we knew, high in heaven, which my Lord gave me, though we could not hold it before the Ruler of all...Yet He has not done right to hurl us into the

35

fiery abyss, to hot hell, reft of the heavenly realm; He has determined to
people it with mankind. That to me is the greatest of griefs, that Adam,
who was wrought from earth, shall hold my mighty throne, dwell in bliss, and
we suffer this torment, affliction in this hell. Alas! had I but the strength
of my hands, and could win free for one hour, but for a winter-hour, then
I with this host...! But around me lie iron bonds, the chain of the fetter
is on me. I am powerless. The hard bonds of hell have seized me so closely.
Here is a great fire above and beneath; never have I looked on a loathlier
landscape; the fire ceases not, hot throughout hell...'

He gets free by black magic.

Is there something about the north, and an island, and the Germanic languages, which might feed that sombre pride in the Satans
of the Caedmon MS and *Paradise lost?*

He recurs in the mystery plays. Here are extracts from the
Coventry cycle:

LUCIFER   A worthier lord forsooth am I
And worthier than he. Ever will I be
In evidence that I am more worthy:
I will go sitten in Gods see   [seat
Above sun and moon and starris on sky.
I am now set as ye may see:
Now worship me for most mighty
And for your lord honoúrè now me
Sitting in my seatè

DEUS   Thou Lucifere for thy micklè pridè
I bidde thee fallè from heavnè to hellè
And all they that holden on thy sidè
In my blissè never more to dwellè.
At my commandèment anon down thou slidè
With mirth and joyè never more to mellè   [mix
In mischief and manas ever shalt thou abidè [menace
In bitter brenning and fièr so fellè
In pain ever to be pight.   [put

ADAM   I dare not touch thy hand for dread
Of our Lord God omnipotent
If I should work after thy rede   [advice
Of God our Maker I should be shent   [By...ruined

Of Goddis wisdom for to lear   [learn
And in kenning to be his peer   [equal
Of thine hand I take it herè
And shall soonè taste this meatè.
Alas! alas! for this false deedè
My fleshly friend my foe I findè.

36

<pre>
            Shamèful sinnè doth us unhedè: [uncover
            I see us naked before, behindè...

            .   .   .   .
EVA   Alas! alas! well-away
            That ever touchèd I the tree!
            I wend as wretched in welsome way: [wild
            In blackè bushes my bower shall be.
            In paradise is plenty of playè,   [pleasure
            Fair fruitès rythè great plentý.   [very
            The gatès be shut with Goddis keyè;
            My husband is lost because of me –
            Levè spousè now thou fondè.   [Beloved spouse that you
                                              are now found to be.
            Now stumble we on stalk and stone,
            My wit away is from me gone:
            Writhe on to my neckè bone   [thump
            With hardness of thy hande...
</pre>

adapted from K. S. BLOCK ed *Ludus Coventriae or The plaie called Corpus Christi: Cotton MS Vespasian D.VIII* EETS 1922

Adam refuses to kill her. The development of personal feelings in the mystery plays comes out well towards the end of the fragmentary Norwich pageant of creation and fall:

> *Then man and woman departeth to the nether part*
> *of the pageant, and man sayeth:*
> Alack, mine own sweetheart, how am I struck with fear
> That from God am exiled and brought to pain and woe!
> O what have we lost? why did we no more care?
> And to what kind of place that we resort and go?

> *Woman*
> Indeed into the world now must we to and fro
> And where or how to rest I cannot say at all.
> I am even as ye are, whatsoever me befall.
> *Then cometh Dolor and Misery and*
> *taketh man by both arms...*

adapted from ROBERT FITCH ed *Norwich pageants: The Grocers' Play* Norwich 1856 communicated to the Norfolk and Norwich Archaeological Society.

The arrival of Dolor and Misery is close to *PL* XI and even closer to Milton's original plans for a sacred drama in which such figures would have had parts.

The 'pageant' in that stage-direction is the wagon. There was one wagon for each Bible story, and those for the creation and fall were particularly elaborate. The bottom part, between the wheels, was hell, furnished with a flaming whale-like hellmouth. The boards of the cart, on which goods would be carried, was 'middle earth', the ordinary world into which Adam and Eve are exiled. Paradise was on a stair or ledge. Heaven was higher still, on a tower, or on the roof of the wagon. In this way the cosmos was actualised. So were the details: the accounts of the Norwich grocers, who acted that play, include items for a 'Rybbe colored Redde' and for the serpent a coat with dyed tights and tail, a wig and a crown.

We think of the mystery plays as remotely medieval. They began early in the 14th century when liturgical drama had been banished from inside the churches; but they were very public, very popular, and highly participatory. They went on being performed well into the 16th century and did not die right out until about 1570 when the secular theatre began. It is worth thinking about the way in which these various elements interact – church:state; church:theatre; play:epic; grocers, cart, street, at Whitsun:poet, bookseller, readers, continuous availability.

Bu the main tradition of religious epic was continental. The religion was of course still the same – the forces of reform had not yet burst out of the Church into protestant churches. But the chief languages were Latin and its descendant Italian, belonging to the Romance group of languages; whereas Anglo-Saxon and Middle English belonged to the Germanic group.

In about 1310 Dante Alighieri produced *La divina commedia*. It was both religious and heroic; patriotic (one of the first ambitious works to be written in Italian instead of Latin), yet allegorical. It opens in a dream, like *Pilgrim's progress* and *Piers plowman*:

Nel mezzo del cammin di nostra vita me ritrovai per una selva oscura, che la diritta via era smarrita.	In the middle of the journey of our life I found myself in a dark wood, where the highway had disappeared.

Dream and allegory are 'romantic' items; yet in *The divine comedy* the Roman epic poet Virgil guides Dante on his journey through the three parts of the poem, *Inferno*, *Purgatorio* and *Paradiso*. That journey involves a visit to the underworld – a standard epic feature; and Dante uses epic similes:

E già venia su per le torbid'onde
un fracasso d'un suon pien di
   spavento,
per cui tremavano ambedue le
   sponde;
	And now across the turbid waves
	came a crash of fearsome noise, at
	which both the shores shook;

non altrimenti fatto che d'un vento	it was a sound as of a wind rushing
impetuoso per gli avversi ardori,	into the hollow of heat, which un-
che fier la selva senza alcun	checked drives into the forest;
rattento;	
li rami schianta, abbatte, e porta	shatters boughs, beats them down
fuori;	and hurls away; then rolling up
dinanzi polveroso va superbo,	dust before it sweeps proudly on,
e fa fuggir le fiere e li pastori.	making wild beasts and shepherds
	flee.
Gli occhi mi sciolse, e disse: 'Or	He loosed my eyes, and said; 'Now
drizza il nerbo	turn your optic nerve upon that
del viso su per quella schiuma	ancient foam, there where the smoke
antica,	is most acrid.'
per indi ove quel fummo è più	
acerbo.'	
Come le rane innanzi alla nimica	As frogs before their enemy the
biscia per l'acqua si dileguan tutte,	snake all scatter through the water
fin ch'alla terra ciascua s'abbica;	till each is squatting on the bottom;
vid'io più di mille anime distrutte	so saw I a thousand and more
fuggir così dinanzi ad un, che al	broken spirits fleeing from the
passo	approach of one who passed over
passava Stige colle piante asciutte.	Styx with soles unwet.

[Canto ix. Approach Dante via the illustrations of Botticelli and Blake.]

Yet that is surely more ghostly, and at the same time more everyday in its details, than Milton's hell? Again, there is no warfare, and no romance – Dante loves Beatrice, and in the poem she is a saint in heaven who guides him at the end to the beatific vision. That vision is of a God invisible except as dazzling geometrical figures 'Nella profondo e chiara sussistenza dell'alto lume' (In the welling bright subsistence of deep light, *Paradiso* xxxiii). Unspeaking, inactive in the plot, he is 'l'amor che move il sole e l'altre stelle' (the love that moves the sun and other stars).

In the 16th century further epics were produced, especially by Italians, which strove to be more heroic than Dante but, at the same time, more religious than Ariosto and Tasso. In particular, these renaissance poets wanted to give epic form to the story of the creation of the world (see 'hexaëmera' in the section on myth above). This was partly because during the 16th century the interest of theologians was shifting from the life of Christ to the fall of man. The creation story also gave writers an opportunity to display their expanding scientific knowledge (creation is an astronomical event), and what they felt about it. The fall displayed the guilt that renaissance man felt, like Prometheus and Dr Faustus, at knowing too much. You can date the importance of creation and fall from Michelangelo's paintings of them on the ceiling of the Sistine Chapel, 1512. Soon after that, Luther and Calvin published detailed commentaries on *Genesis*; in 1568 an Italian poet called Alfani wrote a poem about the *Battaglia celeste tra Michele e Lucifero*; in 1601 the Dutch scholar Grotius wrote a tragedy in Latin on *Adamus exul*; Tasso himself wrote a long poem in lyrical blank verse on *Le sette giornate del mondo creato* (1607). The most typical and influential of these works was *La sepmaine, ou création* (1578), by Guillaume du Bartas, a Huguenot. This was translated into English by a wool-merchant called Joshua Sylvester in 1592–9 as the *Divine weeks and works* and became very popular throughout the 17th century. The first half was about the creation and fall, followed by *La seconde sepmaine* about the entire subsequent history of man. It was an enormous introduction in verse, for the middlebrow, to Christian mythology and doctrine, world history, popular ethics, and the whole corpus of geography, astronomy and science at the time.

Here are extracts from the *Divine weeks* of Du Bartas and Sylvester; and from the three continental works of the 17th century closest to *PL* in content and form:

DU BARTAS *La sepmaine ou création* 1578: trans. SYLVESTER *Divine weeks and works* 1592

> Forming this mighty frame he every kind
> With divers and peculiar signet signed:
> Some have their heads grovelling betwixt their feet
> As the inky cuttles and the manyfeet;
> Some in their breast, as crabs; some headless are,
> Footless and finless (as the baneful hare   [kind of fish
> And heatful oyster), in a heap confused,
> Their parts unparted, in themselves diffused.
> The Tyrian merchant or the Portuguese
> Can hardly build one ship of many trees;
> But of one tortoise, when he lift to float,
> The Arabian fisherman can make a boat;
> And one such shell him in the stead doth stand
> Of hulk at sea and of a house on land.
> Shall I omit the monstrous whirlabout
> Which in the sea another sea doth spout
> Wherewith huge vessels, if they happen nigh,
> Are overwhelmed and sunken suddenly?...
>
> Week 1   Day 5

GROTIUS *Adamus exul* 1601. Hugo Grotius was the international Latin name of a Dutch scholar and reformer. He wrote this tragedy early in life in Latin. Milton stayed with Grotius in Paris in 1638; their education, careers and politico-religious attitudes were similar. Grotius makes much of the love of Adam and Eve, and he makes their dilemmas explicit: for Eve, how can it be wrong to follow her senses, and be natural, and eat the apple? for Adam, how could he abandon her once she has eaten it? Here Eve sees Satan (Act IV, in the translation by W. KIRKCONNELL in his *Celestial cycle* Toronto 1952):

Quod illud animal tramite obliquo means . . . lubricos longos sinus Tendit volumen, terga se in gyros plicant.

> What is that creature, moving with a slantwise path,
> That crawls by winding ways and writhes along to meet me?
> Its flat and scaly head twists back a hissing mouth
> And shakes a three-forked tongue; its two eyes gleam like fire;
> Its rampant neck arises and its clammy breast
> Shines with proud spots; painted with azure markings,
> Its coiling spirals twine, and twist, with hue of gold
> Resplendent; in long slippery volutes it extends,
> And folds its back in many a sinuous labyrinth . . .

Act V Eve sees the flaming sword keeping them out of paradise:

> What sudden gleam is that? What light shines fiercely forth?
> A flame has caught the Garden and the lofty trees
> Are burning without fire, a gleaming conflagration
> That wanders hastily; as when the bright sky shines
> With cometary lights, the whole Grove is ablaze . . .

ANDREINI *Adamo* 1613. Andreini, an Italian, was a professional Biblical dramatist. This is a lively lyric drama of the kind Milton would have seen in Italy. There are many allegorical characters as in Milton's early drafts. Here Adam wakes from the creation of Eve out of his rib (Act I Scene ii in the translation by W. KIRKCONNELL in his *Celestial cycle* Toronto 1952):

> What white and sacred rose in Heaven's garden
> Wet with empyreal dews have I beheld
> Open its bosom to these suns? Or rather,
> What sun emparadised in its soft bosom
> And in a moment after (O high wonder!)
> Rise like a lily in a flood of light
> From the fair virgin breast? Are the suns lilies?
> Are lilies children of the virgin rose?

VONDEL *Lucifer* 1654. Joost van den Vondel, Dutch; trans. W. KIRKCONNELL in his *Celestial cycle* Toronto 1952. Realistic characterization, e.g. Apollyon is a cavalier, Michael a blimp. Strong political and military drama, all taking place in heaven. Vondel was a Roman catholic, a fierce satirist of intolerance, and a scholar. Calvinist criticism forced his play off the stage after two nights but it was successfully revived in 1900. Here Uriel describes the fall of Lucifer:

> As the clear day, turned to insensate night
> When the sun sinks, forgets to shine with gold,
> So all his beauty, in that dread descent,

41

Changed to deformity, accursed and vile:
The heroic visage to a brutish snout,
His teeth to fangs, able to gnaw through steel;
His feet and hands into four sorts of claws;
The skin of opal to an inky hide;
Out of his bristled back burst dragon's wings...

PL and after

So Milton had many options open. When he came to write *PL*, however, he chose an option full of difficulty and conflict: not tragedy, but epic; not romance and patriotism but Christianity. Epic is the most demandingly comprehensive genre; it is also the most authoritative; by it a culture signals that it has arrived at adult power and that its vernacular is fully formed; that is, epic is a declaration of virility and pride. Yet in this epic man admits the folly of his pride and sensuality, submits to God's chastening hand, and leaves the perfect garden.

After Milton, writers were still anxious to produce epics, but the form no longer suited society. Pope planned an epic on Brutus, and translated the *Iliad* and *Odyssey*, but his major work was in mock-epic, *The rape of the lock*, and anti-epic, *The Dunciad*. Wordsworth had heroic ambitions, but his *Prelude*, intended as part of a larger work, drew the tradition into a quite untraditional area, 'The growth of a poet's mind' – epic has become individualized and so turned into something else:

> Not Chaos, not
> The darkest pit of lowest Erebus,
> Nor aught of blinder vacancy, scooped out
> By help of dreams – can breed such fear and awe
> As fall upon us often when we look
> Into our minds, into the mind of man –
> My haunt, and the main region of my song.

Preface to 1814 ed of *Excursion*, quoting end of projected *Recluse* I

A good deal of subsequent literature can be focused from the epic tradition. Keats's *Hyperion* is an unfinished epic of which the hero is the god of a new poetry, perhaps Keats himself. Shelley's *Queen Mab* and his heroic dramas *Hellas* and *Prometheus unbound* are aimed at social and political renewal. *Prometheus unbound* is explicitly related to *Paradise lost*. In the preface Shelley claims that

Prometheus is...a more poetical character than Satan, because, in addition to courage and majesty, and firm and patient opposition to omnipotent force, he is susceptible of being described as exempt from the taints of ambition, envy, revenge, and a desire for personal aggrandisement, which, in the hero of *Paradise lost*, interfere with the interest.

On the other hand, Prometheus spends the poem chained to a rock. That could happen to a major character in lyrical drama like Shelley's, and like Milton was planning originally; but not in epic. So Milton's change of medium changed his message. For further discussion see Goethe, *Faust*, and Byron, *Cain* – both lyrical dramas.

In the same period, Blake wrote a kind of epic called *Milton* (1804–8). The preface attacks the classicism of his time, in the sense of an obligation to imitate classical models:

The stolen and perverted writings of Homer and Ovid, of Plato and Cicero, which all men ought to condemn, are set up by artifice against the sublime of the Bible...Shakespeare and Milton were both curbed by the general malady and infection from the silly Greek and Latin slaves of the sword.

Rouse up, O young men of the New Age! set your foreheads against the ignorant hirelings. For we have hirelings in the camp, the court and the university, who would, if they could, for ever depress mental and prolong corporeal war...We do not want either Greek or Roman models if we are but just and true to our own Imaginations, those Worlds of Eternity in which we shall live for ever in Jesus our Lord.

The song 'And did those feet in ancient time', adopted by the Women's Institutes of Great Britain, follows; then an invocation:

Daughters of Beulah! Muses who inspire the poet's song,
Record the journey of immortal Milton through your realms
Of terror and mild moony lustre in soft sexual delusions
Of varied beauty, to delight the wanderer and repose
His burning thirst and freezing hunger! Come into my hand,
By your mild power descending down the nerves of my right arm
From out the portals of my brain, where by your ministry
The Eternal Great Humanity Divine planted his paradise
And in it caused the spectres of the dead to take sweet forms
In likeness of himself.
............................sitting at eternal tables,
Terrific among the Sons of Albion, in chorus solemn and loud
A bard broke forth: all sat attentive to the awful man.

Much of the poem I don't understand, but it seems to tell of Satan, as the original bright angel, being forced by moral bullying into isolated sinfulness:

his bosom grew
Opaque against the Divine Vision: and paved terraces of
His bosom inwards shone with fires, but the stones becoming opaque
Hid him from sight in an extreme blackness and darkness.
And there a world of deeper Ulro was opened in the midst
Of the Assembly. In Satan's bosom, a vast unfathomable abyss.

43

Milton appears and takes on the form of the Bard, becoming in a way responsible for Satan; and eventually he takes on the desolation of Satan in order to redeem him, very much as in the theory of the atonement Christ takes on the sin of man. It is Milton's bardic redemption of Satan that forces onto him the false classical stiffness:

> And Milton said: 'I go to eternal death! The nations still
> Follow after the detestable gods of Priam, in pomp
> Of warlike selfhood contradicting and blaspheming.
>
> .   .   .   .
>
> What do I here before the Judgement? without my emanation?
> With the daughters of memory and not with the daughters of
>   inspiration?
> I in my selfhood am that Satan: I am that Evil One!
> He is my spectre! in my obedience to loose him from my hells,
> To claim the hells, my furnaces, I go to eternal death!'

During the 19th century, English poets moved away from epic back to romance again – in Tennyson's *Idylls of the King* (i.e. Arthur), Arnold's *Tristram and Iseult* (1852) and his poems on Norse and oriental topics (*Balder dead, Sohrab and Rustum*), and in general the romanticized medievalism of the Pre-Raphaelites and William Morris. You can see from Victorian paintings of classical subjects, and from the classical detailing of their architecture, that even their 'classicism' (and therefore, perhaps, their view of Milton? see Arnold's essay on him) was itself more softly noble, more like a fattening empress, than Milton's. The heroes of Tennyson's classical idylls (*Oenone, Lucretius, The lotus eaters, Ulysses, Tithonus, Tiresias*) admit the temptations of romantic comfort; and Tennyson himself admits it in his poem *Milton*. This is an exercise in classical metre but it manages to make *Paradise lost* feel like the Indian empire on Sunday afternoon:

> ...Milton, a name to resound for ages;
> Whose Titan angels, Gabriel, Abdiel,
> Starred from Jehovah's gorgeous armouries,
>   Tower, as the deep-domed empyrean
>   Rings to the roar of an angel onset –
> Me rather all that bowery loneliness,
> The brooks of Eden mazily murmuring,
>   And bloom profuse and cedar arches
>   Charm, as a wanderer out in ocean,
> Where some refulgent sunset of India
> Streams o'er a rich ambrosial ocean isle...

Shelley defined the epic poet as one 'whose creations bore a defined and intelligible relation to the knowledge and sentiment and religion of the age in which he lived, and of the ages which followed it: developing itself in correspondence with their development' (*Defence of poetry* 1821). It's a wide definition but it will serve as a base from which to consider the epic tendencies of our own century: Eliot's *Waste land*, for instance (1922), and Joyce's *Ulysses* (1921), in which the elaborate imitation of a Homeric structure sets off an anti-hero, Bloom. Poems were written in the 1920s about the materials of *PL*, without pretending to be at all epical or Miltonic – Roy Campbell's *Flaming terrapin* (1924), about the creation, the war and the fall of Satan; *Adam* and *Eve* and various other poems by Rilke (German, trans. Leishman); poems by Edwin Muir on Christian and classical themes; Wallace Stevens, *Sunday morning*; and (later) Karl Shapiro, *Adam and Eve*. But of course those topics no longer held the centrality that they did in the 17th century. What does?

In a poem *To the ghost of John Milton*, Carl Sandburg said that had he suffered what Milton did, 'I would write *Paradise lost*...I would write *Paradise regained*, I would write wild, foggy, smoky, wordy books' (*Good morning America* 1928). Milton was in fact moving towards anti-epic himself. In that sense *PL* was *avant-garde*. He treats most of the traditional elements positively – encyclopedic information, epic similes and so on; but his military hero, Satan, is split off from his culture-hero Adam; and the heroism of both is tainted – Satan the 'author of evil' and defeated, Adam 'our ancestor impure' and expelled. Finally, although the style is certainly grand, its grandeur had then the steely awkward arrogance of a new invention that carries colossal power – a radio telescope for looking at eternity with.

A few texts for studying epic in England

SIR THOMAS MALORY *Morte D'arthur* 1470 from Book XXI

And then King Arthur smote Sir Mordred under the shield, with a foin of his spear throughout the body more than a fathom. And when Sir Mordred felt that he had his death's wound, he thrust himself, with the might that he had, up to the butt of King Arthur's spear. And right so he smote his father Arthur with his sword holden in both his hands, on the side of the head, that the sword pierced the helmet and the brain-pan, and therewithal Sir Mordred fell stark dead to the earth. And the noble Arthur fell in a swoon to the earth, and there he swooned oft-times.

And Sir Lucan de Butlere and Sir Bedivere oft-times heaved him up, and so weakly they led him betwixt them both to a little chapel not far from the sea side. And when the king was there, he thought him well eased. Then they heard the people cry in the field. Now go thou, Sir Lucan, said the king, and do me to wit what betokens that noise in the field. So Sir Lucan departed, for he was grievously wounded in many places. And so as he went, he saw and hearkened by the moonlight, how the pillers and robbers were come into the field to pill and to rob many a full noble knight of brooches and beads, of many a good ring, and of many a rich jewel; and who that were not dead all out, there they slew them for their harness and their riches.

When Sir Lucan understood this work, he came to the king as soon as he might, and told him all what he had heard and seen. Therefore by my advice, said Sir Lucan, it is best that we bring you to some town. I would it were so, said the king.

Chapter v   How King Arthur commanded to cast his sword Excalibur into the water, and how he was delivered to ladies in a barge.

But I may not stand, my head works so. Ah, Sir Launcelot, said King Arthur, this day have I sore missed thee. Alas, that ever I was against thee, for now have I my death, whereof Sir Gawain me warned in my dream.

Then Sir Lucan took up the king the one part, and Sir Bedivere the other part, and in the lifting, the king swooned, and Sir Lucan fell in a swoon with the lift, that the part of his bowels fell out of his body, and therewith the noble knight's heart brast...

GEORGE CHAPMAN trans. Homer *Iliad* 1598–1615
XII 142 Trojan assault on the wall of the Greek beach-head
αὐτὰρ ἐπεὶ δὴ τεῖχος ἐπεσσυμένους ἐνόησαν Τρῶας...

But when the rest had heard
The Troyans in attempt to scale, clamour and flight did flow
Among the Grecians; and then (the rest dismayed) these two
Met Asius entering, thrust him back and fought before their doors.
Not fared they then like oaks that stood, but as a brace of boars,
Couched in their own bred hill, that hear a sort of hunters shout
[sort = party
And hounds in hot trail coming on, then from their dens break out,
Traverse their force and suffer not, in wildness of their way,
About them any plant to stand – but thickets, offering stay,
Break through and rend up by the roots, whet gnashes into air,
Which tumult fills with shouts, hounds, horns and all the hot affair
Beats at their bosoms. So their arms rung with assailing blows,
And so they stirred them in repulse, right well assured that those
Who were within and on the wall would add their parts – who knew
They now fought for their tents, fleet, lives and fame, and therefore
    threw
Stones from the walls and towers as thick as when a drift wind shakes
Black clouds in pieces and plucks snow in great and plumy flakes
From their soft bosoms, till the ground be wholly clothed in white.
So earth was hid with stones and darts – darts from the Troyan fight,
Stones from the Greeks, that on the helms and bossy Troyan shields
Kept such a rapping it amazed great Asius, who now yields,
Sighs, beats his thighs and, in a rage, his fault to Jove applies...

SIR WILLIAM DAVENANT from preface to *Gondibert* 1650

But Tasso, though he came late into the world, must have his share in that critical war which never ceases among the learned [ancients versus moderns]; and he seems most unfortunate because his errors, which are derived from the ancients, when examined grow in a great degree excusable in them and, by being his, admit no pardon. Such are his council assembled in heaven, his witches' expeditions through the air, and enchanted woods inhabited with ghosts. For though the elder poets, which were then the sacred priests, fed the world with supernatural tales and so compounded the religion of pleasure and mystery, two ingredients which never failed to work upon the people, whilst for the eternity of their chiefs, more refined by education, they surely intended no such vain provision. Yet a Christian poet, whose religion little needs the aids of invention, hath less occasion to imitate such fables as meanly illustrate a probable heaven by the fashion and dignity of courts, and make a resemblance of hell out of the dreams of frightened women, by which they continue and increase the melancholy mistakes of the people.

DAVENANT from *Gondibert*
Book II Canto i A description of Verona

> Near to this evening region was the sun
>   When Hurgonil with his lamented load,
> And faithful Tybalt, their sad march begun
>   To fair Verona, where the court abode.
>
> .   .   .   .
>
> An amphitheater which was controlled   [it was which
>   Unheeded conquests of advancing age,
> Winds which have made the trembling world look old
>   And the fierce tempests of the Gothic rage;
>
> .   .   .   .
>
> From wider gates oppressors sally there;
>   Here creeps the afflicted through a narrow door,
> Groans under wrongs he has not strength to bear
>   Yet seeks for wealth to injure others more;
>
> And here the early lawyer mends his pace
>   For whom the earlier client waited long;
> Here greedy creditors their debtors chase
>   Who 'scape by herding in the indebted throng.
>
> The adventurous merchant whom a storm did wake
>   (His ships on Adriatic billows tossed)
> Does hope of eastern winds from steeples take
>   And hastens there a courier to the coast.
>
> Here through a secret postern issues out
>   The scared adulterer who out-slept his time;
> Day, and the husband's spy, alike does doubt
>   And with a half-hid face would hide his crime.

47

There from sick mirth neglected feasters reel,
 Who cares or want in wine's false Lethes steep;
There anxious empty gamblers homeward steal
 And fear to wake ere they begin to sleep.

.   .   .   .

To this vast inn, where tides of strangers flow,
 The morn and Hurgonil together came:
The morn, whose dewy wings appeared but slow
 When men the motion marked of swifter fame...

THOMAS HOBBES (the philosopher) from answer to Davenant 1650

In that you make so small account of the example of almost all the approved poets, ancient and modern, who thought fit in the beginning (and sometimes also in the progress of their poems) to invoke a muse or some other deity that should dictate to them or assist them in their writings, they that take not the laws of art from any reason of their own but from the fashion of precedent times will perhaps accuse you of singularity. For my part, I neither subscribe to their accusation, nor yet condemn that heathen custom otherwise than as accessory to their false religion. For their poets were their divines, had the name of prophets, exercised among the people a kind of spiritual authority, would be thought to speak by a divine spirit, have their works which they writ in verse (the divine style) pass for the word of God and not of man and to be hearkened to with reverence...But why a Christian should think it an ornament to his poem, either to profane the true God or invoke a false one, I can imagine no cause but a reasonless imitation of custom – of a foolish custom, by which a man, enabled to speak wisely from the principles of nature and his own meditation, loves rather to be thought to speak by inspiration, like a bagpipe.

COWLEY from poem to Davenant congratulating him on *Gondibert*

Methinks heroic poesy till now
Like some fantastic fairyland did show:
Gods, devils, nymphs, witches and giants' race,
 And all but man, in man's chief work, had place.

COWLEY from preface to his own *Poems* including *Davideis* 1656

Does not the passage of Moses and the Israelites into the Holy Land yield incomparably more poetical variety than the voyages of Ulysses or Aeneas? Are the obsolete threadbare tales of Thebes and Troy half so stored with great, heroical and supernatural actions (since verse will needs find or make such) as the wars of Joshua, of the Judges, of David, and divers others?

COWLEY from *Davideis* I Hell

Beneath the silent chambers of the earth,
Where the sun's fruitful beams give metals birth,
Where he the growth of fatal gold does see,
Gold which, above, more influence has than he;
Beneath the dens where unfletched tempests lie

48

And infant winds their tender voices try;
Beneath the mighty oceans' wealthy caves,
Beneath the eternal fountain of all waves,
Where their vast court the mother-waters keep
And, undisturbed by moons, in silence sleep:
There is a place, deep, wondrous deep, below
Which genuine night and horror does o'erflow;
No bound controls the unwearied space, but hell,
Endless as those dire pains that in it dwell.
Here no dear glimpse of the sun's lovely face
Strikes through the solid darkness of the place;
No dawning morn does her kind reds display;
One slight weak beam would here be thought the day.
No gentle stars with their fair gems of light
Offend the tyrannous and unquestioned night.
Here Lucifer, the mighty captive, reigns,
Proud midst his woes and tyrant in his chains.
Once general of a gilded host of sprites,
Like Hesper leading forth the spangled nights;
But down like lightning, which him struck, he came,
And roared at his first plunge into the flame.
Myriads of spirits fell wounded round him there;
With dropping lights thick shone the singèd air.
Since when the dismal solace of their woe
Has only been weak mankind to undo...

JOHN DRYDEN trans. Virgil *Aeneid* 1693–7
VI 190 Aeneas in the underworld: the golden bough

vix ea fatus erat, geminae cum forte columbae
ipsa sub ora viri caelo venere volantes
et viridi sedere solo.

  Scarce had he said when, full before his sight,
Two doves descending from their airy flight
Secure upon the grassy plain alight.
He knew his mother's birds; and thus he prayed:

.   .   .   .

  Be you my guides, with your auspicious aid,
And lead my footsteps till the branch be found
Whose glittering shadow gilds the sacred ground.
And thou, great parent, with celestial care
In this distress be present to my prayer

.   .   .   .

  Thus having said, he stopped, with watchful sight
Observing still the motions of their flight,
What course they took, what happy signs they show.
They fed, and, fluttering, by degrees withdrew
Still farther from the place, but still in view;
Hopping and flying, thus they led him on
To the slow lake, whose baleful stench to shun

They winged their flight aloft; then, stooping low,
Perched on the double tree that bears the golden bough.
Through the green leaves the glittering shadows glow;
As, on the sacred oak, the wintry mistletoe,
Where the proud mother views her precious brood,
And happier branches, which she never sowed.
Such was the glittering; such the ruddy rind,
And dancing leaves that wantoned in the wind.
He seized the shining bough with gripping hold,
And rent away with ease the glittering gold.

   .   .   .   .   .

  Obscure they went through dreary shades, that led
Along the waste dominions of the dead.
Thus wander travellers in woods by night,
By the moon's doubtful and malignant light,
When Jove in dusky clouds involves the skies
And the faint crescent shoots by fits before their eyes.

   .   .   .   .   .   .

Full in the midst of this infernal road
An elm displays her dusky arms abroad;
The god of sleep there hides his heavy head
And empty dreams on every leaf are spread.
Of various forms unnumbered spectres more,
Centaurs, and double shapes, besiege the door;
Before the passage horrid Hydra stands,
And Briareus with all his hundred hands;
Gorgons, Geryon with his triple frame,
And vain Chimaera vomits empty flame...

  ...*horrendum stridens, flammisque armata Chimaera,*
Gorgones Harpyiaeque et forma tricorpris umbrae.

ALEXANDER POPE trans. Homer *Iliad* 1715–26
  IV 99 Minerva descends to earth
     Fired with the charge, she headlong urged her flight
And shot like lightning from Olympus' height.
As the red comet from Saturnius sent   [Jove
To fright the nations with a dire portent
(A fatal sign to armies on the plain
Or trembling sailors on the wintry main),
With sweeping glories glides along in air
And shakes the sparkles from its blazing hair;
Between both armies, thus, in open sight,
Shot a bright goddess in a trail of light.
With eyes erect, the gazing hosts admire
The power descending and the heavens on fire...

Iliad XII 424 Action
     The rising combat sounds along the shore
As warring winds, in Sirius' sultry reign,

From different quarters sweep the sandy plain;
On every side the dusty whirlwinds rise
And the dry fields are lifted to the skies;
Thus by despair, hope, rage together driven,
Met the black hosts and, meeting, darkened heaven.
All dreadful glared the iron face of war,
Bristled with upright spears that flashed afar;
Dire was the gleam of breastplates, helms and shields,
And polished arms emblazed the flaming fields.
Tremendous scene, that general horror gave
But touched with joy the bosoms of the brave...

Iliad XXII 453   Achilles defeats Hector

He [Hector] ceased. The fates suppressed his labouring breath
And his eyes stiffened at the hand of death.
To the dark realm the spirit wings its way
(The manly body left a load of clay)
And plaintive glides along the dreary coast
A naked, wandering, melancholy ghost.
Achilles, musing, as he rolled his eyes
O'er the dead hero, thus, unheard, replies:
Die thou the first. When Jove and heaven ordain
I follow thee. He said; and stripped the slain.
Then, forcing backward from the gaping wound
The reeking javelin, cast it on the ground.

.   .   .   .

Then his fell soul a thought of vengeance bred
(Unworthy of itself and of the dead).
The nervous ankles bored, his feet he bound
With thongs inserted through the double wound.
These fixed up high behind the rolling wain,
His graceful head was trailed along the plain.
Proud on his car the insulting victor stood
And bore aloft his arms distilling blood.
He smites the steeds; the rapid chariot flies;
The sudden clouds of circling dust arise;
Now lost is all that formidable air;
The face divine and long descending hair
Purple the ground and streak the sable sand:
Deformed, dishonoured in his native land,
Given to the rage of an insulting throng
And, in his parents' sight, now dragged along.

POPE trans. Homer *Odyssey*
   V 546   Ulysses shipwrecked on Phaeacia

Close to the cliff with both his hands he clung,
And stuck adherent, and suspended hung;
Till the huge surge rolled off; then, backward sweep

The refluent tides, and plunge him in the deep.
As when the polypus, from forth his cave
Torn with full force, reluctant beats the wave,
His ragged claws are stuck with stones and sands,
So the rough rock had shagged Ulysses' hands;
And now had perished, whelmed beneath the main,
The unhappy man; even fate had been in vain;
But all-subduing Pallas lent her power,
And prudence saved him in the needful hour.

  .   .   .   .

That moment fainting as he touched the shore,
He dropped his sinewy arms; his knees no more
Performed their office, or his weary weight upheld;
His swollen heart heaved; his bloated body swelled;
From mouth and nose the briny torrent ran;
And lost in lassitude lay all the man,
Deprived of voice, of motion, and of breath;
The soul scarce waking in the arms of death...

ROBERT FITZGERALD trans. Homer *Odyssey* 1962
  v Odysseus survives shipwreck (continued from above)

      Then the man
crawled to the river bank among the reeds
where, face down, he could kiss the soil of earth,
in his exhaustion murmuring to himself:

'What more can this hulk suffer? What comes now?
In vigil through the night here by the river
how can I not succumb, being weak and sick,
to the night's damp and hoar-frost of the morning?
The air comes cold from rivers before dawn...'

.   .   .   .

He made his way to a grove above the water
on open ground, and crept under twin bushes
grown from the same spot – olive and wild olive –
a thicket proof against the stinging wind
or Sun's blaze, fine soever the needling sunlight;
nor could a downpour wet it through, so dense
those plants were interwoven. Here Odysseus
tunnelled, and raked together with his hands
a wide bed – for a fall of leaves was there,
enough to save two men or maybe three
on a winter night, a night of bitter cold.
Odysseus' heart laughed when he saw his leaf-bed,
and down he lay, heaping more leaves above him.

A man in a distant field, no hearthfires near,
will hide a fresh brand in his bed of embers
to keep a spark alive for the next day;
so in the leaves Odysseus hid himself,

while over him Athena showered sleep
that his distress should end, and soon, soon.
In quiet sleep she sealed his cherished eyes.

POPE trans. Homer *Odyssey*
VII 107 Ulysses comes to the palace and gardens of Alcinous
Meanwhile, Ulysses at the palace waits,
There stops, and anxious with his soul debates,
Fixed in amaze before the royal gates.
The front appeared with radiant splendours gay,
Bright as the lamp of night or orb of day.
The walls were massy brass; the cornice high
Blue metals crowned, in colours of the sky;
Rich plates of gold the folding doors encase;
The pillars silver, on a brazen base;
Silver the lintols deep-projecting o'er,
And gold the ringlets that command the door.
Two rows of stately dogs on either hand
In sculptured gold and laboured silver stand.

   .   .   .   .

Close to the gates a spacious garden lies,
From storms defended and inclement skies.
Four acres was the allotted space of ground,
Fenced with a green enclosure all around.
Tall thriving trees confessed the fruitful mould;
The reddening apple ripens here to gold;
Here the blue fig with luscious juice o'er flows,
With deeper red the full pomegranate glows,
The branch here bends beneath the weighty pear,
And verdant olives flourish round the year.
The balmy spirit of the western gale
Eternal breathes on fruits untaught to fail;
Each dropping pear a following pear supplies,
On apples apples, figs on figs arise;
The same mild season gives the blooms to blow,
The buds to harden, and the fruits to grow...

VOLTAIRE from *Essay upon the epic poetry of the European nations from Homer down to Milton* 1727
It seems that our devils and our Christian hell have something in them low and mean, and must be raised by the hell of the pagans, which owes its dignity to its antiquity. Certain it is that the hell of the gospel is not so fitted for poetry as that of Homer and Virgil.

YVOR WINTERS from *The function of criticism: problems and exercises* 1957
In Homer the gods are more human than divine, and although we may find them primitive in conception, nevertheless they are not supposed to be much more intelligent than Achilles and they mingle in his affairs rather naturally. Milton, however, is concerned with a deity and with additional

supernatural agents who are conceived in extremely intellectual terms: our conceptions of them are the result of more than two thousand years of the most profound and complex intellectual activity in the history of the human race. Milton's form is such that he must first reduce these beings to something much nearer the form of the Homeric gods than their proper forms, and must then treat his ridiculously degraded beings in heroic language.

See further the Chronology at the end of this volume.

Writing, publication and editing of PL

Choice of subject; tragedy or epic

In 1637 when Milton was 28 his mother died. Next year he went to Italy. When he came back, in 1639, he started listing subjects for a big work, in a notebook MS (now in the library of Trinity College, Cambridge). Before going abroad he had been thinking about King Arthur; on return, he still had ancient British legends in mind; and at first it was for a tragedy that he made notes, e.g.

Edwin son to Edward the younger for lust deprived of his kingdom – or rather by faction of monks whom he hated, together with the impostor Dunstan.

Edward son of Edgar murdered by his stepmother; to which may be inserted the tragedy stirred up betwixt the monks and priests about marriage.

Etheldred son of Edgar a slothful king: the ruin of his land by the Danes.

Brightrick of West Saxons poisoned by his wife Ethelburge, Offa's daughter, who died miserably also in beggary after adultery in an nunnery.

Alfred in disguise of a minstrel discovers the Danes' negligence; sets on with a mighty slaughter. About the same time the Devonshire men rout Hubba and slay him.

Harold slain in battle by William the Norman. The first scene may begin with the ghost of Alfred...

Macbeth...

You can see that most of these subjects have themes in common, themes which recur in the poems he actually wrote; and we can ask what his motives might have been. But the main use for such lists is to ask what use has been made of our pre-Conquest history, e.g. by

Shakespeare and Tennyson? And to ask what sort of materials are felt to be heroic or romantic now – Tolkien, Charles Williams, C. S. Lewis? (Tolkien is an Anglo-Saxon scholar; C. S. Lewis was a medievalist and a high Anglican and wrote a book about *PL*.) What sort of subjects did Brecht choose?

It was only in Alfred's reign that Milton thought an epic might be based; his subjects for tragedy ranged wider. He noted many Biblical subjects for tragedy, including the flood, Sodom, Samson, David, Ahab and Jezebel (*II Kings* ix), John the Baptist (cf. Wilde and Beardsley, *Salome*) and the passion of Christ, as well as several versions of Adam and Eve.

He probably wrote some of *PL* as a tragedy. It may have been as early as 1642 that he showed his nephew Edward Phillips, whom he tutored, what is now IV 32–41, the first lines of Satan's address to the sun. He probably did not write much more of the poem for the next fifteen years: they contained two of his marriages, the civil war, his pamphleteering, his government secretaryship. But he had begun to write again by about 1658. He made it up in bed at night, especially in winter, and sent for one of his daughters to 'milk' him and take it down 40 lines at a time. Then he would cut them down to about half, and get his nephew Edward in now and then to go over the MS and correct the spelling and punctuation. The poem was finished by 1665, when Milton lent a copy to Thomas Ellwood, a young Quaker who had recently got to know him. Publication was delayed by the Great Plague of 1665 (when Milton, who had been living near a public burial ground in London, moved to Chalfont St Giles, Buckinghamshire); by the Great Fire of 1666; and by getting the manuscript licensed for publication by the censor (in this case, the Archbishop of Canterbury's private chaplain).

Publication

The first edition of 1667 was sold for 3*s* retail (Donne's poems were selling for 4*s* at the time, and Herbert's for 2*s* 6*d*). Books were published from bookshops – you could get a book only from the bookseller who had bought the author's work and had it printed. Milton's bookseller agreed to pay him £5 down and £5 for each 1,300 copies sold. 1,300 were sold in the first eighteen months – a bit slow but quite a large sale for that time – so Milton got his second £5. In 1674 a second edition was published, with a portrait and this poem by Marvell:

On Mr Milton's Paradise Lost

When I beheld the poet blind, yet bold,
In slender book his vast design unfold,
Messiah crowned, God's reconciled decree,
Rebelling angels, the forbidden tree,
Heaven, Hell, Earth, Chaos, all: the argument
Held me a while misdoubting his intent,
That he would ruin (for I saw him strong)
The sacred truths to fable and old song
(So Samson groped the temple posts in spite),
The world o'erwhelming to revenge his sight.
    Yet as I read, soon growing less severe,
I liked his project, the success did fear,
Through that wide field how he his way should find
O'er which lame Faith leads Understanding blind:
Lest he perplexed the things he would explain
And what was easy he should render vain.
    Or if a work so infinite he spanned,
Jealous I was that some less skilful hand
(Such as disquiet always what is well
And by ill imitating would excel)
Might hence presume the whole creation's day
To change in scenes and show it in a play.

.   .   .   .

    That majesty which through thy work doth reign
Draws the devout, deterring the profane;
And things divine thou treat'st of in such state
As them preserves, and thee, inviolate.
At once delight and horror on us seize,
Thou sing'st with so much gravity and ease;
And above human flight dost soar aloft
With plume so strong, so equal, and so soft;
The bird named from that Paradise you sing
So never flags but always keeps on wing.
    Where couldst thou words of such a compass find?
Whence furnish such a vast expense of mind?
Just Heaven thee, like Tiresias, to requite
Rewards with prophecy thy loss of sight.

What do you think of the anxieties Marvell expresses in the first paragraph? (On the problem of poetry and belief cf. Eliot's essay on Dante; I. A. Richards, *Principles of literary criticism* ch. 35; and W. K. Wimsatt 'Poetry and Christian thinking' in his *Verbal icon* 1954.) Is Marvell wholehearted later on? What exactly are the qualities he points to? The 'less skilful hand' is Dryden's: Milton gave him permission to 'tag his verses' and he produced *The state of innocence and fall of man: an opera* in 1674 (printed 1677). The opening scene

56

Represents a chaos or a confused mass of matter; the stage is almost wholly dark. A symphony of warlike music is heard for some time; then from the heavens (which are opened) fall the rebellious angels, wheeling in air and seeming transfixed with thunderbolts. The bottom of the stage being opened receives the angels, who fall out of sight. Tunes of victory are played, and an hymn sung. Angels discovered brandishing their swords. The music ceasing and the heavens being closed, the scene shifts and on a sudden represents hell: part of the scene is a lake of brimstone or rolling fire; the earth of a burnt colour. The fallen angels appear on the lake, lying prostrate; a tune of horror and lamentation is heard.

Who is being made most fool of? See Bernard Harris, 'That soft seducer, love' in *Approaches to PL* ed Patrides 1968.

To that second edition, of 1674, Milton also made some small corrections; and he raised the number of books from 10 to 12 by splitting the original VII into what are now VII and VIII, and X into XI and XII; he added a few lines at the beginnings of the new VIII and XII.

Milton died later that year. In 1678 a third edition was published. In 1688 a grand fourth edition came out, in folio, with engravings after the Spanish artist Medina, and a new portrait engraving with a poem by Dryden under it:

> Three poets in three distant ages born
> Greece, Italy and England did adorn.
> The first in loftiness of thought surpassed;
> The next in majesty; in both the last.
> The force of nature could no further go:
> To make a third she joined the other two.

That edition of *PL* was one of the first books to be published by subscription. It was a way of ensuring financial backing for expensive volumes; and indicated that *PL* had achieved coffee-table status.

There was a fifth edition in 1692 and a sixth in 1695. Many copies of the sixth had *PR*, *SA* and the minor poems bound in too, so it was a sort of 'poetical works'. It also had extensive notes by an Edinburgh graduate called Patrick Hume who worked as a schoolmaster in England. So *PL* became one of the first annotated editions of any English literature.

Critics and editors

In 1712 Addison wrote essays on *PL* for nearly every Saturday issue of *The Spectator* throughout the spring: see nos. 267 for 5 January 1712, 273, 279, 285, 291, 297, 303, 309, 315, 321, 325, 327, 333, 339, 345, 354, 357, 363 and 369 for 3 May. *PL* was culture. There were several

Of Rainbows and Starry' Eyes. The Waters thus
With Fiſh repleniſh'd, and the Air with Fowl.
Ev'ning and Morn ſolemniz'd the Fifth day.
  The Sixth, and of Creation laſt, aroſe
450 With Ev'ning Harps and Matin; when God ſaid,ǃ
Let th' Earth bring forth *Fowl* living in her kind,   *Soul*
Cattel, and Creeping *things*, and Beaſt of th' Earth, *thing*
Each of their kind. The Earth obey'd, and ſtraight
Op'ning her fertil Womb teem'd at a Birth
455 Innumerous living Creatures, perfect forms,
Limb'd and full-grown. Out of the ground up-roſe,
As from his Lair, the Wildbeaſt where he wons
In Foreſt *wild*, in Thicket, Brake, or Den ;   *wide*
Among the Trees in Pairs they roſe, they walk'd :
460 The Cattel in the Fields and Meadows green:
Thoſe rare and ſolitary, Theſe in flocks
Paſturing, at once and in broad Herds upſprung.
[*The graſſie Clods now calv'd, now half appear'd*
The tawny Lion, pawing to get free

                His

Ѵ. 451. *Let th' Earth bring forth* Fowl *living.*]
A moſt ſhameful Fault here, to have gone through
ſo many Editions. The Author gave it ;
 Let th' Earth bring forth Soul *living in her kind.*
So the Scripture, *living Soul.* Fowl were created
the Day before this.

V. 452. *Cattel, and Creeping* things, *and Beaſt
of th' Earth.*] He gave it, *Creeping* THING, as it is
in *Geneſis* : and thence he adds, *Beaſt* of th'Earth,
not *Beaſts.*

V. 458. *The Wildbeaſt where he wons In Foreſt
wild.*] The *wild* Beaſt in the *wild* Foreſt ? miſera-
ble Jejunity ! The Author gave it,
 The Wildbeaſt where he wons In Foreſt WIDE.

V. 463. *The graſſie Clods now calv'd, &c.*] Here
we are come to a whole Dozen of Verſes, which
are demonſtrably an Inſertion of the Editor's,
without the Poet's knowledge. I ſhall firſt join
together the Lines that are genuine; and their
Connexion will appear ſo inſeparable, that the
Lines intermediate muſt be voted ſpurious; though
they were as elegant, as they'll be found ſilly.

He had ſpoke of the Generations of Beaſts, both
Wild and Tame:
 Thoſe rare and ſolitary, Theſe in flocks
 Paſturing, at once and in broad herds, up ſprung.
 At once came forth whatever creeps the ground,
 Inſect or Worm.
Let any one, either gifted with Poetry, or con-
verſant in good Poets, determine ; if this Repe-
tition, *At once, At once,* did not follow thus cloſe
under *Milton's* forming Stile, nothing interve-
ning. And now let's examine what the Editor would palm upon us. *Quod dedit principium
adveniens?*
 The graſſy Clods now calv'd.
Calv'd is a Metaphor very heroical, eſpecially
for wild Beaſts. But had not the Author ex-
preſs'd it, and much better, before?
 The Earth obey'd, and ſtraight,
 Op'ning her fertil Womb teem'd at a Birth.
Would a Man, that had once ſaid *Teem'd,* have
doubled and polluted it with *Calv'd?* He goe-
on, *The Lion pawing to get free* his hinder parts. The
poor Lion ſtuck faſt in the Paſſage: he wa-
form'd, it ſeems, in the Earth, without any Ca-
vity for him. And his Hinderparts being much
              thinne-

465 *His hinder parts; then springs as broke from bonds,*
And rampant shakes his brinded main. The Ounce,
The Libbard, and the Tiger, as the Mole
Rising, the crumbl'd Earth above them threw
In hillocs. The swift Stag from under ground
470 *Bore up his branching head. Scarce from his mould*
Behemoth, biggest born of Earth, upheav'd
His Vastness. Fleec'd the Flocks and bleating rose,
As Plants; ambiguous between Sea and Land
The River Horse and scaly Crocodile.]
475 At once came forth whatever creeps the ground,
Infect or Worm : those wav'd their limber Fans
For Wings, *and* smallest Lineaments exact ;   *in*
In all the liveries deck'd of Summer's pride
With spots of gold and purple', azure and green :
480 These as a Line their long dimension drew,
Streaking the ground with sinuous trace : [*not all*
Minims of Nature; some of Serpent kind
Wondrous in length and corpulence involv'd

                                                           Their

thinner than his Foreparts; if these were once
out, he needed not to paw and struggle to free
the Hinder ones, which could not possibly stick at
all. But how came out, *Ounces, Leopards, and
Tigers?* one would think, just as the Lion did;
being so near akin in Figure and Strength. No ;
we are mistaken: *They rose up like Moles,* scratch-
ing up Hillocks before them. Weak Tigers in
the Birth, to grow so strong afterwards: And
yet *Milton* had told us, v. 456, that all the Beasts
came out *perfect forms, limb'd and full grown.* But
the swift Stag bore up his branching head. For all
his *Swiftness,* he seems to have lain fast there;
for we hear no more of him beyond his Horns.
Then *the Elephant scarce upheav'd his vastness.*
Scarce upheav'd? with much ado got up? What
an Idiot of an Editor? He confounds the external Force requisite to lift an Elephant, with the
Elephant's internal and natural Force to move
and lift himself. The bulkier he was, the easier
he could *upheave* himself, with a Castle too on his
Back. But he makes us amends at last, *Fleec'd
the flocks and bleating rose, as Plants.* *Milton* had
told us, That the Flocks *at once upsprung in perfect
forms.* The Editor tells us, they had *Fleeces,* for

fear we should think they had been shorn before
they came up. But they *rose like Plants:* so slowly as Plants grow, or *bleating like Plants?* We
will not believe him against *Milton* himself, who
tells us, They *at once* upsprung. He closes the
Scene, with the *Hippopotamus* and *Crocodile,* which
he tells us are *Ambiguous* Animals: but how they
rose, bleating or otherwise; or whether they rose
at all, this Deponent sayeth not: for he has put
no Verb to the Sentence. *Raphael* had rais'd our
Expectation at the beginning,
      What words from tongue of Seraph can suffice?
But surely such Words, such trifling Stuff, were
never put into a Seraph's Mouth, but here.

V. 476 *And smallest Lineaments exact.*] The
Author gave it,
      For Wings, IN *smallest Lineaments exact.*
Exact is the Nominative Case, Insects form'd *exact,*
though in smallest Lineaments. The Microscope
abundantly witnesses that Exactness.

V. 481. *Not all Minims of Nature, some of Serpent kind,* &c.] Our Editor not yet satisfied with
inserting a Dozen Lines, a foolish Description of
      H h 2   his

more annotated editions in the 18th century. The most notable is Bentley's of 1732. Bentley was an eccentric, a great classical scholar and an extravagantly arrogant master of Trinity College, Cambridge. In effect he rewrote the poem to make of it the kind of sense, and the kind of poetry, he wanted. He used the device of saying that everything wrong with the poem was an error due to Milton's blindness, or the folly of an earlier editor. His sarcasm exposes much in Milton's verse which a rationalistic reader cannot accept; and some that most of us accept too easily. On pp. 58-9 is a passage from Book VII where Milton describes the creation of the animals on the sixth day, with Bentley's footnotes.

Further editorial work came out in the two years succeeding Bentley's edition: Zachary Pearce's *Review of the 12 books of Milton's 'Paradise Lost'* in 1733 and Jonathan Richardson, father and son, *Explanatory notes on 'Paradise Lost'* in 1734. Their work, with Bentley's and the initial annotations of Hume, all has a fine querying penetration: they were puzzled by Milton, and sometimes irritated by him. Empson gives an idea of their quality in his essay on 'Milton and Bentley' in his *Some versions of pastoral* 1935 (cf. R. M. Adams, 'Empson and Bentley: *scherzo*' in his *Ikon* 1955).

In 1749 Bishop Newton (Pearce became a bishop too) brought much of the editorial work together; but he was not so sharp as his predecessors and from now on for 125 years the emphasis was on tracking allusions and explaining puzzles. It was only in the 1930s that editors and critics began again to ask what the function of the allusions might be, and whether some of the puzzles might not be muddles on Milton's part instead of the reader's. Not that there was any lack of antagonism to Milton: Dr Johnston wrote a chilly essay on him for his *Lives of the most eminent English poets* which prefaced a uniform edition of their works, in 1779. But the general attitude now was much more respectful and perhaps also more distant, rather as the 18th-century's attitude to God was, compared with the 17th's. The change can be studied in the stanza on Milton in Gray's *Progress of poesy*, an ode which he finished, after long labours, in 1754. Milton appears after Shakespeare; he still has the wing imagery adopted by Marvell, but Gray has none of Marvell's hesitations:

> Nor second he, that rode sublime
> Upon the seraph-wings of ecstasy
> The secrets of the abyss to spy.
> He passed the flaming bounds of place and time:

The living throne, the sapphire blaze
Where angels tremble while they gaze,
He saw; but, blasted with excess of light,
Closed his eyes in endless night.

Almost every phrase is a quotation from *PL*. He is followed by 'Dryden's less presumptuous car'.

In 1801 Archdeacon Todd began to collect the material for a more complete variorum; footnotes were still mainly classical but in 1874 David Masson (professor of English at Edinburgh) started to publish an edition which emphasized Milton's cosmology, his ideas, and his English. In 1891–6 and in 1910 Cambridge University Press published the first edition of *PL* designed for schools, by Verity. It was the most thoroughly annotated of all editions: *PL* had become a set book.

From *Epitaphium Damonis* 1640

I, then, I would tell of Trojan sails along the coast of Kent, and the ancient realm of Imogen...then I would tell of Igraine, whom Uther Pendragon lay with in the countenance and armour of her husband treacherously counterfeit by Merlin, and begot Arthur.

From Trinity College Cambridge MS 1641

Sodom the Scene before Lots gate...the first Chorus beginning may relate the course of the city each evening every one with mistresse, or Ganymed, glittering along the streets, or solacing on the banks of Jordan, or down the stream.

From *The reason of church government* 1642

I began thus far to assent both to them and divers of my friends here at home, and not less to an inward prompting which now grew daily upon me, that by labour and intense study (which I take to be my portion in this life), joined with the strong propensity of nature, I might perhaps leave something so written to aftertimes as they should not willingly let it die.

From *Second defence of the people of England* 1654 on his work as a revolutionary pamphleteer

I have delivered my testimony, I would almost say, have erected a monument, that will not readily be destroyed, to the reality of those singular and mighty achievements which were above all praise. As the epic poet, who adheres to all the rules of that species of composition, does not profess to describe the whole life of the hero whom he celebrates, but only some particular action of his life, as the resentment of Achilles at Troy, the return of Ulysses, or the coming of Aeneas into Italy; so it will be sufficient, either for my justification or apology, that I have heroically celebrated at least one exploit of my countrymen; I pass by the rest, for who could recite the achievements of a whole people?

Ideology

People sometimes ask, 'Well, *did* Milton succeed in justifying the ways of God to men?' I do not think the conversation, if any result, is likely to be profitable. The answer to that question can only be something like this:

Those parts of his belief which stimulated his imagination would receive rich incidental treatment, such treatment as the story of Creation is accorded. But the *solution*, the 'justification of God's ways with men', would read like the record of things thought, not triumph experienced; and so in the main Michael's explanations of doctrine to Adam are, if not perfunctory, uninspired.

That is from *A study in Milton's Christian doctrine* (Oxford 1939 p. 115) by Arthur Sewell. He was one of the most wisely sympathetic critics Milton had had; but his book is not well known, probably because of its title. Sewell also has this to say:

De Doctrina [Milton's Latin prose textbook of theology] and *Paradise Lost* report a mind searching, not altogether easily, for some way of reconciliation between God and man. They are the work of a man whose spirit has been unsettled in his faith in God and his trust in man. They are Milton's attempts to settle a certain quarrel with himself; and the terms of that quarrel are not simple but many. The nature of God plays a large part in it. How can he be omnipotent and we be free? How can he be good and we be evil?...We understand *Paradise Lost* in terms of the conflicts it reports.

54–5...80

Spirit world

Until at latest the Restoration of 1660, most educated people in the western world believed in the existence of God, the Son and the Holy Ghost, and of angels, as personal though spiritual beings. Angels are to us the least familiar characters in *PL*, partly because our images are of androgynous visitors in nightgowns. But that is an 18th-century image; the 17th century thought of angels as male and military. They were also seen in classical uniform – Piero della Francesca's *Michael* in the National Gallery, London, carries a distinctly Roman sword; his general stance is like that of Donatello's *David*, and hence of some classical god or hero such as Hermes or Apollo; his gold halo and white wings seem to belong to the frame or the background rather than to Michael himself. There are some strong classical angels in marble by Michelozzo di Bartolomeo in the Victoria and Albert Museum. This heroic style was more and more reserved, however, to the fallen angels, as you can see from the 1688 edition of *PL* where Medina's

Satan rousing his legions by John Baptist Medina, engraved by Burghers (?). Illustration to Book 1 in the edition of *Paradise Lost* published by subscription in 1688.

Satan is in uniform (plus horns) while the good angels are more gowned and floaty. What we are looking at, presumably, is the history of personifications of good and evil. It is not a simple progression, though: before the renaissance (before, that is to say, Donatello and Piero della Francesca) good angels had also been seen as more feminine (e.g. the *Wilton diptych c.* 1395, National Gallery) and evil angels as more monstrous (see any *Temptation of St Antony*, and Bosch *passim*). But before that again, in the romanesque period of art, good and evil angels were seen as military (e.g. the illustrations to the Caedmon MS). Bad angels are never female, in any period; but they may in a monster period be perversely androgynous, homosexual and so on. So we get a structure of this sort:

When the good angel is	male		he fights or	plays music	in classical uniform
then the bad angel is	male		and fights or	falls, despairs	in classical uniform
When the good angel is	female or androgynous		he fights or	worships	in concealing gowns (perhaps more contemporary than uniform?)
and the bad angel is	monstrous or homosexual		and fights or	tortures	in monstrous or animal shapes

There were seven or nine ranks (degrees, hierarchies, orders) of angels, corresponding to the cosmic spheres, for each sphere was directed by an angel. Angels therefore take on some of the functions of a muse, so far as they produce the music of the spheres. Some painters show them as entirely musical, e.g. the angels playing stringed instruments in Piero della Francesca's *Nativity*; cf. the angels at the end of the scene in heaven in *PL* iii; Milton often associates them with stars, e.g. v 620, 745. The orders were divided into triads:

senior more contemplative		junior more active
Seraphim	Dominations	Principalities
Cherubim	Virtues	Archangels
Thrones	Powers	Angels

Milton does not keep strictly to the hierarchy: Satan addresses his followers as 'Thrones, Dominations, Princedoms, Virtues, Powers' at x 460.

Most details about angels are in V and VIII. But at the end of Book I the fallen angels contract themselves to get into Pandemonium: 'Thus incorporeal spirits to smallest forms Reduced their shapes immense' (789). Incorporeal means unrestricted to bodily form; it does not mean immaterial. They are made of matter, like Adam and Eve (see I 425); but they can become larger or smaller, and more or less solid, change their shape and move with lightning speed, at will, 'By quick contraction or remove' (VI 597).

Cosmology

The world of *PL* was not peculiar to it. It was the world of *Pilgrim's progress*, Donne's poems, Shakespeare's plays; much of it was shared by Chaucer, and 1,500 years before him by Virgil; some of it was shared, and some invented, by Plato 400 BC. But it is pre-modern. As a world-view it ended with Newton. So special study is required. Look at old maps, title pages, and cathedral sculpture such as that over the doors at Chartres and Bourges. Read, at least, *Genesis* i-ii and *Romans* viii; see Plato's *Timaeus* for his creation myth; take some notes from Tillyard, Winny and others in the history of ideas section of the booklist at the end of this book.

Can you articulate your own world-picture? Meanwhile, these sections are merely notes and diagrams.

Diagrams are useful because the renaissance world was schematic, and hierarchical. Things were arranged in shapes as we may arrange numbers in triangles (3, 6) or squares. Their shapes were in fact often based on number, either numbers which are significant in mathematics and music, or numbers with sacred originals, e.g. 3 (Trinity), 7 (scale, Deadly Sins, ages of man, days of week), 12 (apostles) and so on.

Everything had a rank – heaven above, hell below; soul superior to body, reason to appetite, man to woman, gold to lead (lead is a 'base' metal; *base is also a moral word*). All things had a significance which could be pictured in an emblem or used in a metaphysical concept – the lion as king of beasts, the soul a prisoner in the body's cage, a tear an emblem of the globe. To grasp the system, walk through a 17th-century house (e.g. Blickling Hall in Norfolk, which has a ceiling of emblems) and gardens; visit a cathedral (e.g. the west front of Wells in Somerset; the windows of King's Chapel, Cambridge); and look at postcards available at the British Museum.

Books of emblems were specially popular 1590–1640: the first wave perhaps of that pious literacy of the middle class which we still meet in sanctimonious children's stories of the 19th century. The emblem might be a single object already charged with symbolism, in which case the verse moral is little more than a proverb:

Ex *Bello*, *pax.*
To HVGHE CHOLMELEY *Efquier.*

The helmet stronge, that did the head defende,
Beholde, for hyve, the bees in quiet serv'd:
And when that warres, with bloodie bloes, had ende,
They, hony wroughte, where souldiour was preserv'd:
　Which doth declare, the blessed fruites of peace,
　How sweete shee is, when mortall warres doe cease.

GEOFFREY WHITNEY *A choice of emblems* 1585

The objects were often animals, descended from the moralizing bestiaries of the middle ages; e.g. a pelican plucking blood from its breast to feed its ailing young:

Look here and mark, her sickly birds to feed,
How freely this kind pelican doth bleed.
See how, when other salves could not be found
To cure their sorrows, she herself doth wound;
And, when this holy emblem thou shalt see,
Lift up thy soul to him who died for thee...

GEORGE WITHER *A collection of emblems* 1635

66

Or, stronger on ethics than religion, Whitney's mouse:

The mouse, that longe did feede on daintie crommes,
And safelie search'd the cupborde and the shelfe:
At lengthe for chaunge, unto an Oyster commes,
Where of his deathe, he guiltie was him selfe:
　The Oyster gap'd, the Mouse put in his head,
　Where he was catch'd, and crush'd till he was dead.

　The Gluttons fatte, that daintie fare devoure,
And seeke about, to satisfie theire taste:
And what they like, into theire bellies poure,
This iustlie blames, for surfettes come in haste:
　And biddes them feare, their sweete, and dulcet meates,
　For oftentimes, the same are deadlie baites.

Sometimes the emblem would illustrate an anecdote, such as the devil playing bowls (moral: people who frequent places of public amusement find themselves in bad company; Francis Quarles *Emblems* 1633). The story would as often be classical as biblical; mixing the two was not peculiar to Milton in the 17th century. E.g. a picture of Latona (Greek Leto, goddess of night) driving the moon-chariot across the sky with a tidal effect on Neptune as he chases after flying fish on a seahorse:

> The empress of the sea, Latona bright,
> Draws like a lodestone by attractive might
> The ocean streams, which having forward run
> Calls back again to end where they begun.
> The Prince of Darkness had eclipsed Eve's light
> And mortals, clouded in Cimmerian night,
> Were backwards drawn by Eve as in the main;
> 'Twas only Mary drew to God again.
> O chaste Diana, with thy silver beams
> Flux and reflux, as in the ocean streams,
> 'Tis thou canst cause. O draw! and draw me so
> That I in vice may ebb, in virtue flow.

That is by Henry Hawkins, a Roman catholic emblemist (*Partheneia sacra* 1633). He also illustrated a complete garden of Eden in which every detail is emblematic, either from the Bible (garden, tower, portal, fountain, rainbow, olive, palm, bee, dew, dove etc.) or from folklore (phoenix, swan, moon etc.). For Hawkins, the entire garden, and each item in it, is finally emblematic of the Virgin Mary. These are illustrated in Rosemary Freeman *English emblem books* 1948.

You can see the God-given hierarchies becoming man-centred in Pope's *Essay on man* (1732; I iv): most of the correspondences and emblems had decayed, so that later the Romantic poets had to invent their own set for special purposes; Baudelaire has a poem called *Correspondances*; Symbolism, Imagism and Surrealism were attempts to re-charge the world with an original significance. In the 17th century it still had a traditional significance. That significance was not just symbolic, aesthetic; it was moral and religious. It was based on the belief, which Raphael expounds in *PL* v, that all things were created by God and aspire upwards toward him again:

> So from the root
> Springs lighter the green stalk, from thence the leaves
> More airy, last the bright consummate flower
> Spirits odorous breathes...   v 479

68

From Henry Hawkins, *Partheneia sacra* 1633

The World of Paradise Lost by H. F. Hallett. Frontispiece to the edition of
Paradise Lost edited by G. H. Cowling (Methuen, 1926)

As in Donne's *Esctasy*, Milton moves from the scent or 'spirits' of
flowers up through the physiological 'spirits' or fluids of animals to
the spiritual essence of angels.

Some correspondences:

spiritual	human	animal	vegetable	mineral
God	king	lion	oak	diamond

Some hierarchies:

seraph	king	scent
cherub	prince	flower
throne	duke	stalk
		root

The cosmos of *PL* is simple. Above, is heaven or the empyrean (= fiery region), 'undetermined square or round' (II 1048). Its details are based on the New Jerusalem in *Revelation* xxi. Heaven is a place where perfect order produces perfect happiness (as in Plato's ideal state, and in the virtuous soul of Platonism and Christianity).

Below heaven is chaos or the deep, the abyss. It is an infinite welter of primal matter not created into substances. So there is no order; it is the cosmic equivalent of civil war in the state (II 898) or discordant passion in the soul. Neither does it admit of up or down.

Hell lies as it were at the bottom of chaos, enclosed by a vault like a dungeon but with one pair of gates, where Sin and Death keep watch (II 644).

At creation, God scooped a hollow out of chaos and in it formed the world by putting some of the 'dark materials' of chaos into created shape ('world' in *PL* = universe). The world hung from heaven by a golden staircase leading to an aperture in its outer shell (III 501) and a passage through the spheres. It is through this hole that Satan enters at III 526; and to it that Sin and Death build their causeway through chaos, so linking the world to hell as well as heaven:

> in little space
> The confines met of empyrean heaven
> And of this world, and on the left hand hell
> With long reach interposed.   x 320

Astronomy

Earth, centre of the universe, is stationary. The moon, sun and planets revolve round it in their spheres. Their spheres are sometimes thought of simply as their orbits, more often as transparent globes in which they are set. Beyond them the 'fixed' stars – i.e. not planets – are set in one special sphere, which also revolves, very fast (v 176). Then comes the crystalline sphere (hyaline), a transparent globe of liquid designed to insulate the universe (VII 270). Its swaying or 'trepidation' explains the precession of the equinoxes (III 483; Donne *Valediction forbidding mourning*). Finally the Primum Mobile or 'first moved' (III 483) is a hard outer shell, the 'outer convex'. God, the First Mover, moves it, and it moves all the other spheres in sympathy, producing the apparent movements of stars and planets, sun and moon; and also producing the music of the spheres.

All the space between the outer sphere and the sphere of the moon was filled with 'ether', the purest of substances (hence 'ethereal sky'

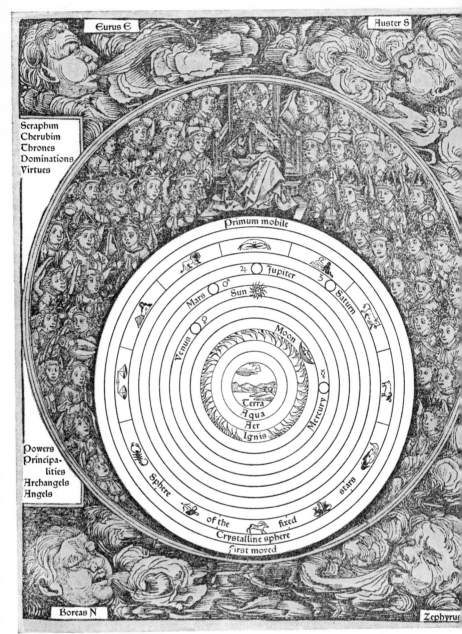

Renaissance cosmos adapted from the *Nuremberg Chronicle* 1493

etc. at I 45, V 267 418 and 'ethereal substance' etc. at II 139, III 716, VI 330, VII 244). Above the moon's sphere, all was eternal; but sublunary things are subject to change (like the 'dull sublunary lovers' love' in Donne's *Valediction forbidding mourning*).

The regularity of the stars was a model of obedience for men, for the microcosm – the 'little world of man' as an individual and as a 'body politic' – should imitate the macrocosm:

> if the celestial spheres should forget their wonted motions and by irregular volubility turn themselves any way as it might happen...what would become of man himself, whom these things now do all serve? See we not plainly that obedience of creatures unto the law of nature is the stay of the whole world?

RICHARD HOOKER *The laws of ecclesiastical polity* 1594; cf. Ulysses in *Troilus and Cressida* I, and *PL* V 153–208 hymn to creation, 618–27 dance of angels and stars, VII creation of the world

This system was called Ptolemaic, after the 2nd-century Alexandrian astronomer Ptolemy, who worked on earlier proofs that the earth is round. Milton outlines it at VIII 66–178, together with versions of the Copernican system, and reference to the more modern Galileo. (Copernicus was a Pole who *c.* 1530 proposed that the sun, not the earth, was at the centre; but all these astronomers are worth looking up for yourself in an encyclopedia.)

Psychology

For every macrocosm there is a microcosm. Man is a model of the cosmos. He is composed of body and soul (see Donne's *Holy sonnet* 'I am a little world made cunningly'). Like all other things, the body is composed of the four elements, fire, air, water, earth. If they are in the right proportion, the man will be healthy and equable.

'That divine particle of God's breathing, the soul' (*Reason of church government* Bohn ii 499) consists of reason or understanding; will; and appetite or passion. For peace and efficiency, the appetites should apply to the will, as motive-force, to be satisfied; and the will should be guided by the reason (VIII 635).

The appetites, stimulated by the senses, are the part of man most closely related to animals. The reason is the part of man closest to God and the angels; but it has to work discursively, by logic, whereas the angels' reason apprehends the truth intuitively.

If there had been no fall, man would have developed into an angelic being. Then he would have understood everything intuitively,

73

without having to work it out (v 493–500); he would have become a psychosomatic whole with no distinction between body and soul (VIII 622–9); and he would have become invulnerable because his life would not have been localized but diffused – 'Vital in every part' (VI 44–7). [To understand these virile spirits, see Tintoretto's *St Michael with a donor*, Lorenzo Lotto's Gabriel in his polyptych at Ponteranica, and the angels in Tiepolo's *Flight into Egypt, Abraham and the angels, Christ in the garden of olives*. Consider also the use made of them in other poetry of the 17th century, e.g. Donne *Air and angels*, Vaughan *Childhood, Corruption, The retreat*, Traherne *Wonder* and Lord Herbert of Cherbury *Platonic love*.]

Sin occurs when the appetites instead of the reason direct the will. At the fall, this condition became habitual:

> Understanding ruled not, and the will
> Heard not her lore, both in subjection now
> To sensual appetite, who from beneath
> Usurping over sovereign reason claimed
> Superior sway.   IX 1127

Since then, the reason has been dimmed; and the will has become infected so it may defy reason: 'all corrupt, both mind and will depraved' (x 825). But education can help the reason 'to restore the ruin of our first parents' (tract *Of education*); and God's grace helps the will if the sinner is repentant.

There is something of a muddle in Milton's psychology, or rather in the orthodoxy that he used. The emphasis on obedience and will starts before the fall, when you would expect the system to be self-regulating. Raphael warns Adam,

> take heed lest passion sway
> Thy judgement to do aught which else free will
> Would not admit.   VIII 635

This muddle is inherent in the myth: the notions of perfection, of free will, and of a test of obedience with the apple, are not really compatible; hence the Father's logic-chopping – 'I made him just and right, Sufficient to have stood though free to fall...Not free, what proof could they have given sincere Of true allegiance, constant faith or love...?' (III 98). After the fall the emphasis is on an understanding of God's plan, and an obedience to his will, which one might think impossible for fallen man. The theory was that God had revealed his plan in the Bible, and Christ had fulfilled obedience (XII 401–4) so that faith in him, and the grace that was then returned, made righteousness possible; but there is no doubt that Milton emphasized the active, deliberate elements of salvation – will, obedience, fortitude, 'strenuous liberty' – more than the receptive emotional elements of faith and love.

Ethics

Milton's chief ethical interest was freedom. He wanted to be free of his own appetites, and the appetites of others, especially tyranny. Repeatedly he says you can't have the second freedom without achieving the first; and since the fall that is difficult:

> Since thy original lapse, true liberty
> Is lost, which always with right reason dwells
> Twinned, and from her hath no dividual being:
> Reason in man obscured, or not obeyed,
> Immediately inordinate desires
> And upstart passions catch the government
> From reason, and to servitude reduce
> Man till then free. Therefore since he permits
> Within himself unworthy powers to reign
> Over free reason, God in judgement just
> Subjects him from without to violent lords.   XII 83

'Right reason' = conscience, intuition of divine truth. This does not prevent Milton blaming tyrants, and those who submit to tyranny: they magnify in politics the fallen state of the soul. Samson scorns the Israelites, 'By their vices brought to servitude...to love bondage more than liberty, Bondage with ease than strenuous liberty' (269). So we reach one of the central paradoxes of *PL*, that Satan justifies himself as a rebel who has a case against tyranny: Mammon tells the peers of hell to prefer 'Hard liberty before the easy yoke of servile pomp' (II 256). The only answer to this is Abdiel's, that to rebel against God, 'whose service is perfect freedom', is the cause of the worst slavery, slavery to oneself: 'Thy self not free, but to thy self enthralled' (VI 181). The old question stands, though: whether the poem makes God's service *feel* as free as Satan's rebellion? We are likely to agree with Blake in *The marriage of heaven and hell* that Milton 'Was of the Devil's party without knowing it', at any rate in a limited sense: although Satan is desperately selfish, he displays initiative, energy, intelligence which we must admire. We could be released from our admiration if the powers of heaven were more attractive in a different way; but on the whole they are not very

75

attractive, and they often oppose Satan's force with what feels like the same kind of force raised to omnipotence. We could also be released if there were a genuine renunciation of all worldly power, as in *Ash Wednesday* and *Four quartets*; the love of Adam and Eve comes close to this – beside it, at the end of *PL*, Satan seems irrelevant; but the poem as a whole is itself too magnificent a celebration of Milton's own knowledge and art and determination for us to accept it as a renunciation of turbulent human striving.

Theology

For the serious Christian no 'good' act is worthy unless the whole life be God-directed. Therefore turning away from God is the prime wrong. The rebellion of Satan, the vanity of Eve, the disobedience of Adam, are all magnified rejections of God. Because they reject God, the elements of good in them cannot count – Satan's courage, Adam's loyalty to Eve. This is the crucial difference between humanistic ethics, and religion. Eliot explains it in *Gerontion:*

> Think
> Neither fear nor courage saves us. Unnatural vices
> Are fathered by our heroism. Virtues
> Are forced upon us by our impudent crimes.

Christian humanism

Milton was, however, a 'Christian humanist': at his time, this meant one who, though he believed man to be sinful, respected the dignity of man and his central position in the universe. He also tried to dedicate the noblest secular goods to God's service, especially learning and art. He wanted to set up theatres for plays and recitations 'to imbreed and cherish in a great people the seeds of virtue and public civility, to allay the perturbations of the mind, and set the affections in right tune' (*Reason of church government*). He urged freedom of the press against a 'cloistered virtue' (*Areopagitica*). He believed, as was normal, that the best classical literature, though pagan, was beneficial as art; and he could not resist acquiring scientific knowledge (he is supposed to have visited Galileo in confinement). His respect for secular knowledge and classical art made him uncomfortable at times, as it did Herbert for example (see *The agony*, *Vanity*, *The pearl*). In *PL* especially, the most obviously classical art falls on Satan's side; and when Adam asks Raphael about the structure of the universe, Raphael has to warn him,

> Solicit not thy thought with matters hid,
> Leave them to God above, him serve and fear.   VIII 167

This is partly because the fall consists in eating an apple of the Tree of Knowledge.

In *PR*, Christ does reject all knowledge and power except God's:

> he who receives
> Light from above, from the fountain of light,
> No other doctrine needs, though granted true.   IV 288

Christ also rejects all art except the Hebrews': the Greeks

> loudest sing
> The vices of their deities, and their own
> In fable, hymn, or song, so personating
> Their gods ridiculous, and themselves past shame.   IV 339

This view was put forward by Plato, and it was fairly common in the 17th century; but it could only produce discord in an epic poet.

Puritanism

Milton was also a puritan. This does not mean that he was puritanical in the sense of disapproving of bodily pleasures – he drank wine and smoked a pipe – or of sex: he married three times, and wrote several pamphlets urging easier divorce, and even polygamy; he believed we have a right to enjoy 'the faultless proprieties of nature' in physical and spiritual love; he believed those kinds of love were inseparable from each other. His puritanism was much more spiritual and political than behavioural. On the spiritual side, he hated the Roman catholics and distrusted the Anglicans because he thought that vestments, candles, prayers to the Virgin and saints, liturgies, ecclesiastical decoration, distracted attention from the inward life of the spirit, and from the one God. Like many people, he saw Christian ritual as a return to the polytheism and idolatry that Moses and King Josiah and St Paul had struggled against. Politically, a powerful priesthood, with legal powers to compel attendance at church, suggested the tyranny and hypocrisy of the pharisees; and they intruded between the worshipper and God. Bishops might enforce conformity (as Archbishop Laud did) by fines and imprisonment; at worst they would sell the country back to the Pope and reintroduce the stake.

The general motive of nonconformity is always the same: to get back to simple forms of worship; to concentrate on the individual's direct relationship with God; and to imbue the whole of his life, not just his time in church, with religion. Many nonconformist sects

77

developed in the 17th century; the strongest were the Presbyterians, who nearly took England over. Milton saw that nonconformists could be as tyrannical as an established church: 'New presbyter is but old priest writ large' (sonnet). In the end Milton left all sects and was a Christian individualist.

Here is a passage from the beginning of Milton's prose pamphlet, *The reason of church government urged against prelaty* (1641–2). In it you can see how liberally his ideas ranged between discipline and 'vagancy', reason and happiness, harmony and energy:

Nor is there any sociable perfection in this life, civil or sacred, that can be above discipline: but she is that which with her musical cords preserves and holds all the parts thereof together...

And certainly discipline is not only the removal of disorder but, if any visible shape can be given to divine things, the very visible shape and image of virtue, whereby she is not only seen in the regular gestures and motions of her heavenly paces as she walks, but also makes the harmony of her voice audible to mortal ears. Yea, the angels themselves, in whom no disorder is feared, as the apostle that saw them in his rapture describes, are distinguished and quarternioned into their celestial princedoms and satrapies according as God himself has writ his imperial decreee through the great provinces of heaven. The state also of the blessed in paradise, though never so perfect, is not therefore left without discipline, whose golden surveying reed marks out and measures every quarter and circuit of New Jerusalem.

Yet is it not to be conceived that those eternal effluences of sanctity and love in the glorified saints should by this means be confined and cloyed with the repetition of that which is prescribed: but that our happiness may orb itself into a thousand vagancies of glory and delight and with a kind of eccentrical equation be, as it were, an invariable planet of joy and felicity. How much less can we believe that God would leave his frail and feeble (though not less beloved) church here below to the perpetual stumble of conjecture and disturbance in this our dark voyage, without the card and compass of discipline? Which is so hard to be of man's making that we may see even in the guidance of a civil state to worldly happiness, it is not for every learned, every wise man, though many of them consult in common, to invent or frame a discipline. But if it be at all the work of man, it must be of such a one as is a true knower of himself, and in whom contemplation and practice, wit, prudence, fortitude and eloquence, must be rarely met, both to comprehend the hidden causes of things, and span in his thoughts all the various effects that passion or complexion can work in man's nature; and hereto must his hand be at defiance with gain, and his heart in all virtues heroic. So far is it from the ken of these wretched projectors of ours that bescrawl their pamphlets every day with new forms of government for our church. And therefore all the ancient lawgivers were either truly inspired, as Moses, or were such men as with authority enough might give it out to be so...because they wisely forethought that men would never quietly submit to such a discipline as had not more of God's hand in it than man's.

Here is an example of Milton's puritanism in action (*Of reformation* the opening of the pamphlet):

Sad it is to think how that doctrine of the gospel, planted by teachers divinely inspired, and by them winnowed and sifted from the chaff of overdated ceremonies, and refined to such a spiritual height and temper of purity, and knowledge of the Creator, that the body, with all the circumstances of time and place, were purified by the affections of the regenerate soul, and nothing left impure but sin – faith needing not the weak and fallible office of the senses to be either the ushers or interpreters of heavenly mysteries, save where our Lord himself in his sacraments ordained: that such a doctrine should, through the grossness and blindness of her professors, and the fraud of deceivable traditions, drag so downwards as to backslide one way into the Jewish beggary of old cast rudiments, and stumble forward another way into the new-vomited paganism of sensual idolatry – attributing purity or impurity to things indifferent that they might bring the inward acts of the spirit to the outward and customary eye-service of the body: as if they could make God earthly and fleshly because they could not make themselves heavenly and spiritual. They began to draw down all the divine intercourse betwixt God and the soul, yea, the very shape of God himself, into an exterior and bodily form, urgently pretending a necessity and obligement of joining the body in a formal reverence and worship circumscribed...But to dwell no longer in characterising the depravities of the church, and how they sprung, and how they took increase: when I recall to mind at last, after so many dark ages wherein the huge overshadowing train of error had almost swept the stars out of the firmament of the church, how the bright and blissful Reformation by divine power struck through the black and settled night of ignorance and antichristian tyranny: methinks a sovereign and reviving joy must needs rush into the bosom of him that reads or hears, and the sweet odour of the returning gospel imbathe his soul with the fragrancy of heaven.

Miltonic concepts

Milton shared most of his ideas with other writers and thinkers of the time, of course. A glance at Donne's sermons will show that his favourite subjects for preaching were angels, the creation of the world, hell and the soul. But here is a list of references in *PL*, and occasionally in the prose (Bohn ed), where Milton expresses what were some of the most important concepts for him:

Reason

Reason versus passion VIII 588 607 635, IX 1125, XII 82.
Reason as liberty XII 82 cf. *PR* II 466.
Reason as love VIII 579, IX 240.
Reason and the Son V 609, VI 43.
Reason and force VI 40.
Reason as maze, error II 558, X 830.

Liberty

Man born free. *Tenure of kings and magistrates* (ii 8–9): 'No man who knows aught can be so stupid to deny that all men naturally were born free, being the image and resemblance of God himself; and were, by privilege above all the creatures, born to command and not to obey.'

Liberty versus bondage with ease II 255, IV 946 957, V 782, VI 166. *Of reformation* ii 401. Cf. *Samson passim*, espec. 270–1.

Liberty and discipline VI 789; *Of reformation* ii 441.

Freedom of speech *Areopagitica* espec. ii 95.

Obedience and acceptance

Obedience to bad ruler VI 174.

Obedience to God II 860, IV 80, V 501 821, VI 740, VIII *passim*, IX 1140 IX 288 561; cf. end of Dr Johnson's *Vanity of human wishes*.

Free will

III 99 ff., IV 65, V 235 520, VI 227 689, VIII 588, X 9 43, XI 351 *Areopagitica* ii 74.

Love

IV 513 774, V 539, VIII 170 182. *Doctrine and discipline of divorce* espec. first 7 chapters (Bohn iii).

Angels, spiritual life

I 424, III 244, V 493, VI 158 345 435 594 660, VI 590, VII 156, VIII 613 625, IX 708 882, XI 61.

Recurring themes in Milton

The last sections have been about Milton's conscious ideas. Other concerns lie below that level, and of course spread from work to work. Consider some of these:

The structure of space and time as plastic stuff: *Vacation exercise*; Satan in chaos in the latter part of *PL* II; other angelic journeys in *PL*; creation in VII; effects of sin on the cosmos in X.

How things work: the universe as a machine; *felix culpa* (the fortunate fault), atonement, grace, as a machine? Gates, organs, smelting, cannons, stomachs. *Nativity ode* stanzas 7, 12; *PL* I *passim*, hellgates in II, end of IV, the war in VI, creation in VII, technology again in XI; *Reason of church government* ii 498 *Of reformation* ii 397.

Harmony and discord: *Nativity ode* 93–140 *L'allegro* 144 *Solemn music,*
Comus, *PL* v 652, xi 552 *Education* iii 475–6. This theme relates to
the next –

Orpheus: *Il penseroso* 103 *Lycidas* 58 *PL* vii 32. See essay that follows.

Disguise, deceit, nets, mazes, snares, mists, wandering, error, hypocrisy,
false shame: *Comus*; *PL* ix (Satan's entry into paradise as mist, etc),
xi–xii (wandering); *PR* i–ii; Delilah in *Samson*; 'those mazes and labyrinths
of dreadful and hideous thoughts' in *Of reformation* (ii 417).

Darkness–light, eyes, inner and outer illumination: *L'allegro* and *Il penseroso*;
eyes, sun etc. in *Lycidas*; *Comus*; invocations in *PL*; *Samson*; *Of reformation*
often e.g. ii 367 387–8; *Apology* iii 147; *Animadversions* ii 70.

Towers, pillars, sceptres, thrones, chariots, idols etc: *PL* i–iii vi *PR* iii.

The following extract from a 2nd-year undergraduate's essay
exemplifies the study of recurring themes in Milton.

from *Orpheus, music and noise: a structural motif of PL*

by JOHN DORLING East Anglia

...*Paradise lost* is an attempt to record the 'one true history' (Prof. Sir
Walter Raleigh *Milton* 1900), with equal stress on the unity, the truth
and the historicity; the unfallen world is of necessity explained in the
terms and references of the fallen; but the parallels and similes given
to this purpose are not strictly metaphorical. Metaphor is in a sense
irrelevant since all these are but ectypes of the archetype: *PL* is the
derivate, the ur-myth – in the imaginative, not obviously the anthropologists' sense; all spring from the original fall.

So, we might say, the Orpheus myth in *PL* is one of many ectypes,
a pale reflection of some aspect of the one true history. On one level,
this is so: there is no good above God, no man above Adam, no evil
above Satan, but our fallen condition constrains us to contemplate
such divinity, evil and humanity through ectypes; in a word, we
cannot take it neat. But there is more than one level to it. Orpheus is
not mentioned much as Orpheus, but, hoping to avoid the stigma of
intrusion, I want to suggest that the Protean figure of Orpheus and the
sound of music, which is his sign, cast their shadow and harmony over
PL in a significant way. Others might shoot other motifs to promi-
nence; this is indicative of the onion-skin nature of the poem's
structure, at once a great virtue and a great failing of *PL*.

The Orpheus myth was much used, and in many ways, during the

16th and 17th centuries.[1] From the classical and medieval references available, 16th-century Italian poets had formulated the Ideal Shepherd, an untutored sage, a true but disappointed lover, a type of the Golden Age.

Orpheus was invoked to justify the wedding of Christianity and Platonism; on the evidence of the Orphic Hymns, he was seen as a founder of religion, and the figure of the minstrel–theologian helped explain the relation of music and philosophy. A proto-humanist, he it was who charmed wild nature and preached the fruits of civilization.

The Italian adaptation was further adapted in England, where Orpheus might be found without footnotes in books about love, music, rhetoric, music, education and in all kinds of songs and poems. The artist–civilizer–sensuous lover formed a curious but harmonious whole. Some thought the poet was the father of lies, but Orpheus was called in to prove them wrong: poetry civilized.

The figure is not unrecognizable in the dense, modern prose of Marcuse: Orpheus, and Narcissus, are the opposite of culture-heroes such as Prometheus, who represents the repressive 'performance principle':

These archetypes envisioned the fulfilment of man and nature, not through domination and exploitation, but through release of inherent libidinal forces.[2]

In our civilization, we experience the 'distortion of the aesthetic attitude into the unreal atmosphere of the museum and Bohemia'; in the reconciliation of Eros and Thanatos accomplished by substitution of Orpheus and Narcissus for false culture-heroes, order means beauty, work means play.

But there is another part of the tale, forgotten by the renaissance men and Marcuse, but remembered by Bacon. Having lost Eurydice, Orpheus roamed the desert (still charming), until the Thracian women he had spurned came screaming and blowing cornets, and (what is particularly important to PL) thus drowned the harp's harmony so that the order it brought to Nature was restored to Chaos; in the confusion, he was dismembered, his limbs strewn and his head cast in a river. (The dismemberment of Truth, and its painstaking reassembly, in the figures of Osiris and Set and Isis, was a preoccupation of

---

[1] A full list of references will be found in K. R. R. Gros-Luis, 'The Triumph and Death of Orpheus' *Rice University Studies in Eng. Lit.*, Winter 1969. See also MacCaffrey *PL as myth* and Campbell *The hero with a thousand faces*.

[2] H. Marcuse *Eros and civilisation* 1956 ch. 9, cf ch. 8 on Orpheus and Narcissus.

Milton himself.[1] Mrs MacCaffrey believes this to have been his conception of the work of *PL*.) Bacon saw Orpheus as the 'image of philosophy'. His music represented 'natural philosophy', 'the renovation of contemptibles...the appeasing of infernalities'; his charming power was moral or civil philosophy. Orpheus had brought order from nature and in communicating it, bridged the gap between art and philosophy. But even wisdom must pass; the fury must come; if it continues 'a barbarous age must follow'. On the same wavelength as Milton in the passage just mentioned, he felt that only a few fragments of 'philosophy' would be found after the dismemberment of Orpheus, until one day they break out again somewhere else, like the Lesbian oracle.

The death and dismemberment were stressed more and more into the 17th century. In some cases, the Orpheus figure took on a static, antique aspect, and was sometimes treated contemptuously. Consistent with this is the increasing isolation of the poet-figure; in this age of discord and noise, Orpheus might no longer charm man or beast; the song is sung for its own sake. We are familiar with the sense among Metaphysical poets that language has lost its innocence, words are treacherous in a world where vices are virtues, virtues vices (see for instance George Herbert's *Jordan I* or Donne's *Women's constancy*). References to Orpheus' death are in justification of poetry itself in despite of public distrust. The vice is inspired; the severed head cannot be silenced.

Gros-Luis suggests that, in the succession of Milton's poems, the decline from renaissance super-optimism to the sombre isolation of the mid-17th century in the use of Orpheus is reflected in miniature. The progression brings us to *PL* VII 30–9, the only point in the whole work where 'the Thracian bard' is mentioned directly (apart from a brief reference at III 7, on which more below). The poet's position is not so much identified with that of Orpheus, as set off by the resonances sounded by the introduction of that Protean figure.

[1] The following comes from *Areopagitica* and is quoted by MacCaffrey: 'Truth indeed came once into the world with her divine master, and was a perfect shape most glorious to look on: but when he ascended, and his apostles after him were laid asleep, then straight arose a wicked race of deceivers who as that story goes of Egyptian Typhon with his conspirators, how they dealt with the good Osiris, took the Virgin Truth, hewed her lovely form into a thousand pieces, and scattered them to the four winds. From that time ever since, the sad friends of Truth, such as durst appear, imitating the careful search that Isis made for the mangled body of Osiris, went up and down gathering up limb by limb still as they could find them. We have not yet found them...nor ever shall do, till her Master's second coming.'

He was divinely inspired, he charmed hell, and was reserved a place in heaven; the poet of *PL* also seeks divine aid in accomplishing 'things unattempted yet in prose or rime'. But has he got it? Might not his be the presumption of fallen man to depict the unfallen world? In a sense, Orpheus is a part of that latter world, the Golden Age; Milton is not. Orpheus' Muse could not save him, but Milton cannot even be sure of his own Muse's patronage. The anxiety is still there: the latter's 'heavenliness' set against the former's 'emptiness' might be seen as whistling in the dark.

This constant questioning of the truth value of myth runs counter to the immense imaginative use made of its resources.[1] It is perhaps a matter of didactic form to frown from time to time on fable: as long as you only do it in the odd half-line or so that wanders away from the main body of discourse, after you have tapped its power to the full. In the above instance, at least, that odd half-line also has a dramatic function. The 'barbarous dissonance'[2] is the antithesis of that true, unfallen harmony both poet-figures seek to communicate, and not only communicate, but create – Orpheus is the charmer; it is the antithesis of the harmony of creation as it was, and of the true voice of poetry. The fact that it was made by the Bacchantes lends the undertone of misgiving at that fatal female power that could lead man to fall. Here is Mr Gros-Luis (on this passage):

The poet is isolated; beset by death and dissonance, charming woods and rocks, but not men. Again, the Muse cannot protect her son.

And he concludes that the passage indicates the increasing decline of the idea of the triumphant Orpheus, who, as the 17th century drew on to its close, became more and more of a stereotyped, commonplace figure, not recreated but referred to. In tracing the history of one figure and the concepts related to it, he is concerned to show a steady progress, or rather decline, in which Milton is one more milestone.

I don't mean to suggest that he is wrong: what he says about the Urania passage seems broadly true; but it is not *all* that is true about

---

[1] But cf. Giles Fletcher *Christ's victory and triumph* epicted by MacCaffrey:

> Who hath not seen drownèd in Deucalion's name
> (When earth his men and sea had lost his shore)
> Old Noah? and in Nisus' lock the fame
> Of Samson yet alive? and long before
> In Phaëton's mine own fall I deplore;
> But he that conquered hell to fetch again
> His virgin widow by a serpent slain,
> Another Orpheus was than dreaming poets feign.

[2] I note the same phrase is used of the raving followers of Hecate who distend the 'rural minstrelsy' of the Spirit (*Comus* 549).

84

it. In tracing one line of decline, he perhaps discounts the back-trackings and eddies so embarrassing to all linear historical theories; because, in a sense, *all* the echoes that cling to the name of Orpheus are caught up in the poem *PL*. That is why we have bothered to summarize them; and our glance at the Urania passage should hint at its central importance: the tremendous train of suggestion it sets off reaches backwards and forwards through the 'half...yet unsung'. If he appears in person once only, his presence is felt throughout in the concepts associated with him. Literature fixes, but myth resounds, changing its shape and import continually. So within the great formal structure of *PL*, the volatile substructure of the Orphic myth insinuates itself into our consciousness.

On the face of it, we might be inclined to suspect the contention that wherever there is music (or its antithesis) and musical figures in *PL* there is a manifestation of Orphic myth; but, in effect, this is what I am suggesting. The use of the concord–discord motif is strikingly consistent with many of the features of Orpheus we have mentioned. This is not to deny the substantiveness of that motif in itself, but to suggest another and, I think, an enriching, level of appreciation.

The relation of concord–discord is woven into a basic scheme of continual comparison, cross-reference and ironic set-off between heaven and hell and paradise. The fallen angels have their own fine music to charm their steps over fire and inspire them to heroism; but this, set as it is amidst the more obviously hellish reminders of noises of various degrees of unpleasantness, serves to recall the heaven of their origin. The music of hell is piped or trumpeted; flutes are not employed at all in heaven; the trumpet is, but as a 'heroic' gesture; heroism is not the part of heaven but of hell and fallen man. But let us allow for the moment that we are gulled by the fineness and inspirational quality of the music in *PL* I and II. We shall hear again the 'warlike sound' of 'sonorous metal blowing martial sound' in the battle in heaven; we shall recognize it as having already been established as the music of hell, and this strengthens the effect sought, which is this: that at the moment of rebellion, Satan created hell and introduced it to heaven; the *place* hell doesn't exist chronologically but it has been created imaginatively in I and II, and we recognize its signs: both the more obvious sheer noise – 'horrid shock...clamour; such as heard till now was never...clashing brayed Horrible discord ...dire was the noise of conflict...the dismal hiss of fiery darts' (VI 206) and so on; and also in the heroic trumpery, the parades and clarion-calls. The noise of their rout has risen to crescendo so that finally 'confounded Chaos roared' (871). The parade of the good angels is thus more of a parody of the Satanic parade than vice versa.

Likewise, Pandemonium rises to the sound of music; like Thebes to Amphion's lyre, says Fowler pertinently, for this is a species of diabolic Orphism: music charms stone and gold, but not only that: it orders them, civilizes them into the forms of architecture. In the creation, 'angelic hymning' accompanied each day's work, rising to a crescendo at the sixth day, while Adam and Eve, in their own small Orphic way, charm nature into voicing praise. As Eve says, without Adam there is no Eden; so without him it is not charmed. But as regards the glory of Pandemonium, true to pattern, diabolic glory is deflated; the castle parodies the forms of earthly and divine order: it is subsequently dismissed, so casually, as 'strawbuilt citadel'.[1]

And so all the sweet music – and there is sweet music in hell, as well as the noise of drum and cymbal – the trumpeting pageantry, the cheers and heroism is finally reduced in the same way. The harmony that, again in a diabolic Orphean way, 'suspended hell and took with ravishment the thronging audience', is metamorphosed into the 'dismal universal hiss' of x 508–75; the whole passage bristles with s sounds. Thus parody is not allowed the status of parallel...

Harmony is the basis of the unfallen world. God charmed nature and so ordered the universe, and that sings back to him: the angels, the spheres, the birds, animals, even the water of paradise, and Adam and Eve, each encouraging the other. Adam, then, is master of his 'happy rural seat'; he charms it and it charms him. The music of Eden is suitably 'natural': birdsong and murmuring stream, consistent with the exclusively vegetarian, submissive animal world (strange that man should impute his guilt at killing animals onto animals that kill other animals; but, we forget, this is a charmed world: only man has the intelligence that registers guilt in our world; the animals of paradise are 'subtle' too, as Eve says; they are marked by the original sin; they fall too). In the 'nuptial bower', the nightingale 'all night long her amorous descant sang'. As we have remarked, the universe is united in song, and so 'heavenly choirs the hymenean sang' as well. The voices of Adam and Eve are also 'naturally' musical, 'more tuneable than needed lute or harp to add more sweetness'. We can see that instruments would be out of place in paradise; they belong to

[1] I 773. Milton is never quite convincing in his deflation of diabolic aspirations. The aspirations themselves remain far more memorable than the little ironic indicators. The fact that overall the parody backfires in this way leads to serious doubts on the reader's part as to the whole status of Satan. But discussion of this artistic flaw would require another essay.

the technological world of Jubal and Tubal Cain.[1] Naturalness and simplicity require to be stressed; the tremendous complexity of the organ fugue so well conveyed at XI 560 ff evolved *as a result of* the fall, of man's *having to conquer* a hostile environment, and dig out, burn and bend raw materials as the devil Mulciber did in hell. In Eden, at least, prevails that right relation between man and nature that Orpheus embodies: 'not to irksome toil but to delight He made us' (IX 242). A Marcusean sentiment, if ever there was one.

But there is another, Bacchantean kind of charm in paradise. In paradise scenes, it occasionally happens that a word is used in a quite innocent sense, but at the same time carries undertones which look forward in an ominous, yet unobtrusive way to the fallen sense. So it is with Eve's 'charm'; in the above passage it is more openly suspicious; in an earlier scene it seemed less so:

> he in delight
> Both of her beauty and submissive charms
> Smiled with superior love.   IV 496

Even here, though, her charms and Adam's smile are immediately followed by Satan's 'leer malign'. The misgivings at this mysterious female force (VIII 530 ff) which is both yielding and overpowering look backwards to hell and the

> uxorious king, whose heart though large,
> Beguiled by fair idolatresses, fell
> To idols foul
>
>   I 445 note the thump on 'fell'

and forwards to the fallen world and the 'bevy of fair women, richly gay In gems and wanton dress' (XI 582). The fatal word again appears in the split second before Adam eats the fruit and is lost. The warnings are realized: 'But fondly overcome with female charm.'

And so earth groans at the fall of Adam and Eve,[2] and the first thunder crashes in place of the last song. Nature is involved in man's corruption; as discord in nature was the counterpart of Orpheus' death, so is the fall of man to earth's groan. The world must be re-ordered on a fallen basis (x 650 ff deals with this, at inordinate length).

---

[1] I have not been able to deal with the various kinds of music and instruments; I find the flute particularly fascinating in *PL*.

[2] Knowing little and understanding less of 'numerology' I don't quite know what significance should be placed on the fact that this last pause before the storm of the fall occurs at line 999 of Book 9, the universal groan then commencing at the round number of line 1000. At any rate, it seems more than sheer coincidence.

The misgiving of Adam at female power and its connection with the noisy dismemberment of Orpheus is also, as we have remarked, shared by the poet-figure. The poet descended chaos and returned 'with other notes than to the Orphean lyre', but this real trial, unlike Orpheus', is in heaven; in a sense, he fell off Pegasus in surrender to the Bacchantean power he feared yet felt attracted towards, in making the fallen world too attractive, for all its discord.

Recurrent words in PL

You often find words recurring in a poem, e.g. *dark, time, past, future* in Eliot's *Four quartets*. Certain key words recur in *PL* with great frequency. The classic study is of the word *all* in *PL* by William Empson in his *Structure of complex words:*

My count gives 612 uses of the word in the poem, or about once every seventeen lines...The poem is about all time, all space, all men, all angels, and the justification of the Almighty. But Milton was already using it in his typical way in *Comus*. It seems to be suited to his temperament because he is an absolutist, an all-or-none man...It is as suited to absolute love and self-sacrifice as to insane self-assertion...The vowel is the 'organ' note for which Milton is praised, or the Virgilian moan at the sorrow inherent in the whole. Thus the word has a good many connections with the whole theme of the poem, though its meaning remains very simple...one can almost say that Milton uses *all* whenever there is any serious emotional pressure. The puzzling question comes after admitting this: to what extent do all the different uses enrich each other; do they all, when you are at home in the style, get coloured by one key sentiment or covert assertion?

That particular recurrence (the phonetic sign for the vowel is [ɔ]) starts with the first lines of the poem:

> Of man's first disobedience, and the fruit
> Of that forbidden tree, whose mortal taste
> Brought death into the world, and all our woe

Most of the words associated with it there also recur. The group *fruit, tree, taste, appetite* and their associates is especially worth checking on, e.g. at IV 194–251 (paradise), V 51–85 (Eve's dream anticipating the fall), V 333–41 (getting dinner for Raphael), VII 531–46 (creation), VIII 304–27 (God's instructions to Adam), IX *passim* (temptation and fall), X 550–65 (Satan's parody-punishment).

Here are a few of the stranger cases in this complex:

to their supper *fruits* they *fell*   IV 331

It is supper; but the previous line ends with the word *appetite*; is it a sort of warning?

> So saying, with dispatchful looks in haste
> She turns, on hospitable thoughts intent
> What *choice* to *choose* for delicacy best,
> What order, so contrived as not to mix
> *Tastes*, not well joined, inelegant, but bring
> *Taste* after *taste* upheld with kindliest change...   v 330

Eve going to cull fruit. But why so much repeating emphasis?

Book IX's recurring words and patterns need to be studied in more detail; but note how often there *fruit* is associated with *false* (e.g. 1011, 1070) and hence with *fall*, *fault* etc. That pattern is repeated of Satan when he returns to hell – 'With what permissive glory since his fall Was left him, or false glitter' (X 451) and at XI 413, 'that false fruit'. What kind of a use of language is this? Cf III 95–130, the poem's theological centre.

There are many other cases. You might notice the epithets that Milton uses of the tree of knowledge and its fruit – *defended, interdicted* etc. at XI 86 426, IX 904, X 554, V 52, VII 46, IX 645. They don't seem to be merely variations on the phrase 'forbidden tree'; but what larger effect might they have?

Other verbal patterns worth considering in *PL* (not necessarily the most numerous, but effective) centre on *hand*, especially for Adam and Eve (IV 488 689 739, V 17, VIII 300, IX 385 780 850 892 997 1037, XI 276 421, XII 637 648); *sit* in the debate in Pandemonium in II; and *waste, wide, wild, wilderness, world, wander, err*: I 60, III 424 633, VII 20 50 212 302, VIII 333, X 283, XI 283 487 627, XII 224 313.

As a further example of the kind of work that might be done in this area, here is part of another 2nd-year East Anglia essay.

from *The fall as process* by
JIM GOWLAND East Anglia

...If one agrees with Huxley that a belief in God is irrational, and that to say 'that God is ultimate reality is just semantic cheating, as well as being so vague as to become effectively meaningless',[1] then the relevance of original sin will evaporate in theological terms. Yet this poem is crammed with symbols that anthropologists can trace far beyond. The anxieties that surrounded the change from fruit to meat are traceable in the poem's concern with food-gathering. Adam

[1] J. Huxley *Essays of a humanist* 1964.

and Eve are aware that paradise is so plentiful that the fruit 'uncropped falls to the ground' and as they sleep 'the flowery roof Showered roses' on them: after the Fall the gift in Adam's hand is destroyed:

> From his slack hand the garland wreathed for Eve
> Down dropped, and all the *faded* roses shed   IX 892

Before the Fall the environment blesses them, as its petals float down onto their bodies; after the Fall the words *down, dropped, shed* denote the harshness that is come...

The fall-as-process describes the way in which Milton develops the notion of 'rising' associated with 'goodness' and 'falling' often associated with 'badness'. The impact of the word *fall* itself is increased by the subtle way words, which have the vowel changed, carry similar changes of meaning. Replacing *a* in *fall* with the remaining vowels produces *fell, fill, folly, full.*

Although *fell* suggests that the Fall has taken place it is used with great force when Eve relates her dream. The dream purports something in the future, yet *fell* suggests that it is already chronicled in her imagination or in God's register of the past and future:

> My guide was gone, and I, methought, sunk down,
> And *fell* asleep;   V 90

The ambiguity about 'fell asleep' being both the action of going to sleep and 'falling *whilst* asleep' places the suggestions about the fall in the reader's mind five books before the actual temptation. Again the importance of Satan's fall into hell (symbolizing man's fall later), is pointed out by the play on the tenses of falling. The word *befall* here means not only 'happened', but *be fell*, in a state of falling:

> Say Goddess...what *befell* in heaven
> To those apostates, lest the like befall
> In paradise   VII 45

When in the same account Lucifer loses heaven, *fell* is given a greater impact by its suggestion of direction: 'Lucifer from heaven...*Fell* with his flaming legions through the deep Into *his* place' (VII 135). The word is made all the more strong by the notion that it ends with him falling into his place, he fits in like a ball into its net.

The word achieves enormous strength when, a mere paragraph before the end of Book XII, Eve returns to the idea that she 'fell' in a dream, in an unthinking, unconscious dream: 'With sorrow and heart's distress Wearied, I *fell asleep*' (XII 615). The word *fell* here reverts to its real tense, the past. Before 'the fall' she dreamed that she fell *while* asleep; wearied and sorrowful she returns again and again to the fall – for in her dreams 'I fell. Asleep'. At the end of Book x the idea that they will always remember the Fall, the original sin, is shown when they pray: 'They...prostrate *fell* Before him reverent, and both confessed' (x 1100). We get the sense that 'they fell even *while* prostrate' – enhanced by the stillness of their pious position juxtaposed with the ideal of falling, as a violent motion.

The other words that suggest *fall* also appear throughout the poem, helping to weave a complex fabric. In hell for instance the very first time the 'fallen' angels came into contact with the material substance of hell's floor they contaminate it, they make it 'fall':

in even balance down they light
On the firm brimstone, and *fill all the plain*   I 350

They gently fly down; and, as if by magic, they infect the brimstone and make the plain fallen...When Eve is being tempted, Satan describes how he saw the fruit on the tree and got into the tree: 'to pluck and eat my *fill* I spared not' (ix 595). As a perversion of whole-some eating this is hard to better. Adam and Eve have eaten with Raphael – where the notion of 'eating one's fill' is quite appropriate. Here the Devil is covering his evil intent with a wholesome natural image – and of course means that he 'ate my *fall*'. *Fill* again means that the Fall immediately filled his body. Thus by packing the ideas of fall and fill into this one word, we get the notion that by eating she will *at once* be both fallen and filled up – completely fallen.

Structures in PL

Conventional structures and episodes

By the 17th century certain large structural conventions had been established for epic. Conventions need not be used conventionally. They can hold a work into the tradition while the poet applies the details freshly, pulling the tradition into his own time. But by the time *PL* came to be published, the whole tradition was in jeopardy. The 17th century admired classical models, as you can see from its painting and building; but there were writers now, in the latter half of the century, who thought the classics (especially Homer) should not be imitated, or even respected: they were fictitious, heathen, and, with so much athletic prowess, divine lust and animal sacrifice, vulgar. We have already seen Cervantes, and Milton himself, mocking another part of the tradition, romance; and so far as it was positive, romance was about to be taken over by novelists anyway. As for Christianity, it has obviously been weaker ever since the Restoration than it was before, both as a national religion and as an element in literature. Some people thought that Christian materials should not be used in epic in case they were made to look ridiculous – there are hints of that in Marvell's poem on *PL*; it is a defensive attitude. Finally, a good deal of what had attracted renaissance poets to this material had lost its attraction. Satan's indomitable will seems to belong more to the world of Marlowe than to Dryden's. The sense of proud individual value, and fierce individual guilt, that marks Faustus and Donne and the puritans, is not a characteristic of the Restoration. Above all, perhaps, a universe which God created in concentric spheres, and poets could celebrate with magnificent theological metaphors, and scholars could understand with little telescopes, was giving way to infinite space comprehensible only to mathematicians and physicists. There were no unicorns or phoenixes in it and if there had been they would not have been reverenced as emblems of virginity and the resurrection, but stuffed and put into a glass case. (This is a complicated business. See Willey *17th-century background* ch. 7, 8, 10; Broadbent *Some graver subject* ch. 1, section 3; M. M. Ross *Poetry and dogma*.)

Milton nevertheless wrote his Christian epic, against the tide; and some of the conventions of structure in *PL* run against the tradition too, or start a new one. Here is a list of the chief structural elements:

Invocation of a muse or dedication to a patron. Milton's muse is Urania, or the Holy Spirit (I, III, VII, IX). Each of his invocations is partly a prayer, and more personal than the rest of the poem. They could be considered as a group, together with renaissance paintings of Apollo and the muses (e.g. by Raphael and by Poussin) and the general question, what is 'inspiration'?

A hero. As in some Elizabethan plays, there is a villainous hero. He drops out after Book X; yet Adam does not enter till IV. These peculiarities force on us such questions as, Who do I admire? What makes a culture hero?

Beginning *in medias res*, with the earlier part of the story told in a flashback (V-VII; cf. *Aeneid* II-III). Is it boring to begin at the beginning?

Councils of the gods about the fate of mortals. Milton uses these to expound theology in III, X, XI; cf. the debates in hell at II and X. How do politics fit theology? It is hard to see redemption as an act of policy; but what about subversion?

Descent of the gods to sway human efforts: Satan in IV, good angels in V and XI, and Son and Sin and Death in X.

A *parade* of troops, catalogue of ships, etc. Milton turns his, at I 392, into a review of comparative religion.

A great *battle*. V-VI.

A *voyage*. Milton uses Satan's voyage from hell to the world in II-III, and back again in X.

Visit to the *underworld*. This is usually part of the voyage but Dante makes a whole book out of it; Milton starts with it, and returns to hell briefly in X.

A *pastoral* interlude where the hero is refreshed and tells his story, and may fall in love. This convention was elaborated in the romantic epics and there were sometimes two pastoral paradises, one an evil temptation (Spenser's Bower of Bliss, *FQ* II xii) and the other ideal (Gardens of Adonis, *FQ* III vi). *PL* IV-VIII.

Perilous encounters with *monsters*, witches, etc. – Beowulf in Grendel's cave, Odysseus with the Cyclops, Aeneas meeting Cerberus in Hades, Spenser's Mammon's Cave and Busirane's castle in the *Fairy Queen*, and so on. Milton uses this convention only in the description of hell in II, and the appearances of Sin and Death in II and X.

Sacrifices and prayers to the gods. Cf. *PL* X-XI.

Games, tournaments and other social rituals. Briefly at II and IV; dancing at III.

A *feast*, followed by song. Cf. Adam and Eve's dinner with Raphael in V; the angels feast in heaven in V also.

Cosmology, astronomy, geography and other sciences. *PL* V and VIII especially; and the general scope of the poem.

Vision: sometimes of the future, especially the future glory of the race. Dante uses the beatific vision, the sight of God, in the *Paradiso*; Milton approaches this in III. Books XI-XIII consist of a vision of the entire history of the world.

At the end, the *return* of the hero to his home, or arrival at his destination, or his death. *PL* peculiar in being open at the far end when Adam and Eve leave paradise.

For interpretation of all these, see the Epic and Mythology section of the booklist at the end of this volume.

All these conventions relate an epic to its predecessors. Some of them also relate it to its own time, its audience and their interests. Milton typically uses them to define Christianity. His invocations are prayers for divine inspiration – he is a priest-poet, likening himself to Moses 'who first taught the chosen seed, In the beginning how the heaven and earth Rose out of chaos'. By making Satan the hero of the first half of the poem, Milton fulfils the convention of grand, aggressive heroics but in IX condemns it in favour of 'the better fortitude of patience and heroic martyrdom'. Satan's voyage through hell and chaos, 'fraught with mischievous revenge' (II 1054), condemns adventurers who sail to exploit 'the puny habitants' (II 367). Milton's science is serious and up-to-date: in VIII, Raphael admits that the earth may orbit the sun. The vision of the future in XI-XII goes far beyond any classical epic, to the last judgement. The poem opens at the end into this fallen world.

Some of the conventions are for entertainment, especially the battles, games and feasts. Milton tried too hard with these: military and social entertainment does not suit his myth; the rebel angels with their gunpowder are, as he knew, absurd. It is a failing of Christian mythology, that its vital parts do not include violence, physical prowess and gaiety. These elements are available, as in the stories of David; but they are mostly in the Old Testament and not central to the myth. In XI, Milton tries to make up for this lack by elaborating the flood and other violent incidents far more than *Genesis* does: the authors and performers of the medieval mystery plays had similarly humanized and roughened many Biblical episodes, including some in the gospels. But there is not much solid secular activity untainted by sin in *PL*:

the unwieldy elephant

To make them mirth used all his might, and wreathed
His lithe proboscis.   IV 345

This is a pity, for Milton's talent was for muscular activity. He is able
to exercise it, though, on the 'good' side, in Book VII about the creation
of the world. The whole book is a kind of hymn in praise of nature:

on smooth the seal,

And bended dolphins play; part huge of bulk
Wallowing unwieldly, enormous in their gait
Tempest the ocean.   VII 409

The heavens and all the constellations rung,
The planets in their stations listening stood,
While the bright pomp ascended jubilant.   562

Some of the conventions tie the poem and its audience into deep
history and the accumulated experiences of humanity. The roll-call
of troops is like a genealogy, tracing society's ancestry: Milton
condemns human pride by calling a roll of idols. The voyage, the
visit to the underworld and encounters with monsters stand for phases
in every human life: the struggle towards a destination (perhaps
adulthood itself), hampered by nightmare troubles and siren voices;
one of the reasons we take Satan's side is that his voyage is ours.
Adam's life in Eden stands for another phase, 'that happy garden
state' of childhood (Marvell *Garden*), or the warm peace of being in
love, 'The voice of the hidden waterfall And the children in the
appletree' (Eliot *Little Gidding*). These are archetypal patterns of
human experience. In *PL* their religious function often obscures their
human import but sometimes we can glimpse it, as when, through
Satan's feet, we re-experience our own kind of hell – 'uneasy steps
Over the burning marl' (I 295); or meet the Terrible Mother in Sin;
or in Adam and Eve see all lovers – 'Thus talking hand in hand alone
they passed' (IV 689).

The question always to ask about these conventions is, How does
Milton adapt the convention? Does it suit his kind of epic, especially
his Christian theme? And does it still work for us? The general
answer is that he puts into each convention – indeed, into the whole
epic – more than it will hold; so there is plenty to work for us, but it
is awkward to handle. Homer's catalogue of ships becomes an essay
in anthropology; Milton's underworld is the classical hades, Mt Etna,
the Christian hell, Dante's inferno, and the fearsome landscape of
romance, all in one; it is also, like everything in Milton's poem, *the*
underworld, the only true one of which all others are imitations.

Symbolic action

It sometimes helps in a long poem to consider what a part of it is symbolically *doing*, and what that action symbolizes within the whole. For example, Book I obviously begins with a hovering action, then a smashing dive into hell, then a heaving up, scurrying to and fro, digging, building and finally secure concealment as the devils get off the lake of fire, construct Pandemonium, make themselves small and go inside. Book III starts by going up and up to heaven, ends going down and down to earth. Book VII has distinct actions – putting, planting, spreading, budding, emerging; the actions of IX are also distinct but quite different.

You can also think of ritual actions designed unconsciously to deal with conflicts in the self, with fears, with gods and demons and enemies. For example, the invocation at the beginning of Book III, when Milton moves from the hellish to the heavenly area, might obviously be regarded as a purification ritual; the invocation at VII propitiates the gods for daring to write about heaven; the punishment of Satan in X exorcizes him from the poem. At a more complicated level you can ask what it may mean to conduct some of the large-scale operations of *PL*, such as exploring the abyss, flying between worlds and worlds, constructing a universe, defeating the rebels. What are we doing for ourselves when we privately fantasy such actions, or their analogues?

Structural patterns

The structural patterns of *PL* are simple and bold; but they can be overlooked because we are not used to looking for them. There seems to be no official word for the device, though it is familiar in novels. For example, in Lawrence's *Sons and lovers* the basic pattern is this:

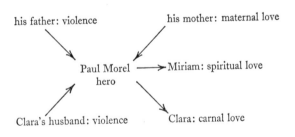

Other patterns are woven through this basic one. Paul is deeply aware of natural things – butterflies, the moon, wild flowers – but his first job is in a factory that makes surgical appliances.

When this kind of parallelism and cross-reference occurs in *PL*, it lacks the naturalness which the leisurely intimate detailing of a novel can give. The result is that we may feel it to be unfair, as if determining *from outside* that Clara shall be full-blooded, red, illuminated, while Miriam must be tendersweet, dark and antiseptic as pine; or that hell shall be dark, violent, technological, while heaven is bright, peaceful and natural.

Anyway, here are some of the structural patterns in *PL*, arranged in the main areas of the poem:

Heaven	*Paradise*	*Fallen world*	*Hell*
VI 507 Founding cannon in war in heaven		XI 560 Jubal Cain	I 700 Founding ore for Pandemonium
III Council of redemption		XI 657 Council	II Council of war
V Council of the Son			V Council of war
VI Council of war			X Council
X Council of judgement			
XI Council of redemption			
			I 43 Fall of Satan
			II 993 Fall of Satan
			III 560, 739 Descents of Satan
IV 555 Descent of Uriel			
	IV 172 Satan enters paradise		
V 257 Descent of Raphael			
	V 275 Raphael enters paradise		
	IX 48 Satan enters paradise		
X 85 Son descends	and enters paradise		
XI 126 Michael descends	XI 228 Michael enters paradise		

Heaven	Paradise	Fallen world	Hell
	XII 639 Adam and Eve descend from paradise		
Father, Son, Holy Ghost	Adam, Eve		Satan, Sin, Death (see II 761, 868; X 399)
Creation in VII	Sin and Death's causeway from hell to earth in X (bringing hell into universe)		Monstrous landscape in II
War in V–VI (bringing hell into heaven)			
		XI 634 war (bringing hell onto earth)	
River in heaven	Rivers in paradise		Rivers in II
Agape or charity, e.g. III 142 'Love without end and without measure grace'	Love of Adam and Eve, e.g. IV 492, 736		Satan's rape of Sin II 761
		IX 1034 sex after the fall	
		XI 569 sons of god and women	

There are many more of these parallels. The most important pattern of all is the one in which the Son's offer of himself as sacrifice for man's sin is echoed by Adam and by Eve in penitence:

> Behold me then, me for him, life for life
> I offer, on me let thine anger fall;
> Account me man...   III 236 and see XI 32

>   that all
> The sentence from thy head removed may light
> On me, sole cause to thee of all this woe,
> Me, me only just object of his ire.   X 933 and see X 773

Typology

That echo is Milton's own version of a traditional way of relating different parts of Christian myth to each other, especially the Old and New Testaments. It is called typology. A person or event in the Old Testament might be seen as a type (or 'antetype') of one in the New. So Christ is the second Adam of *I Corinthians* xv, the 'greater man' of *PL* I 4. Typology was especially a visual device: see the windows of Chartres Cathedral and King's College, Cambridge. Of smaller works, an enamel altarpiece (originally a pulpit) of Nicholas of Verdun, at Klosterneuberg (reproduced in Floridus Röhrig *Der Verduner Altar* Vienna 1955; slide at University of East Anglia) illustrates Christ's fulfilment of the law in panels like this:

17 panels before (approx.) the law of Moses	OT
17 panels in the life of Christ	NT
17 panels after (approx.) the law of Moses	OT

Here is a set which appears to be about the visits of royalty:

Melchisedech visits Abraham	*Genesis* xiv
The Three Kings visit Christ	*Matthew* ii
The Queen of Sheba visits Solomon	*I Kings* x

At a more profound level it is about the powers of earth and heaven acknowledging the genealogy of Christ. In literary terms, the effect is metaphorical: the Queen of Sheba is an image or 'figure' of the Three Kings, as Solomon is of Christ; and so on. The parallels of content may be crude, e.g. Joseph in the well, Christ in his tomb, Jonah in the whale; but in that case the parallels of design are subtle. Each panel is dominated by a vertical: behind the well a tree, beyond the tomb a palm, above the ship a mast. So we move into the field of emblems, where any kind of tree or even pole may suggest the cross. Another part of the altarpiece of Nicholas of Verdun (*c.* 1180) shows Eve plucking the fruit from the tree; the Marys taking Christ's body from the cross; and Joshua's men taking down the body of the hanged king of Ai (the title says Jericho but that's a mistake: *Joshua* viii). From this all sorts of parallels and causal relationships arise, e.g. Eve = Mary; Christ = fruit; Tree of Knowledge = Cross; victory over Ai = victory over sin. It justifies Eliot's use of the Hanged Man from the Tarot pack as a vague metaphor for Christ.

Another small work, which can be inspected easily, is the Alton Tower triptych in the Victoria and Albert Museum (4757–1858). It shows:

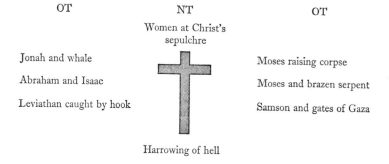

OT	NT	OT
	Women at Christ's sepulchre	
Jonah and whale		Moses raising corpse
Abraham and Isaac		Moses and brazen serpent
Leviathan caught by hook		Samson and gates of Gaza
	Harrowing of hell	

What is the typological structure? For further study see André Grabar *Christian iconography: a study of its origins* 1969 and Rosemond Tuve *A reading of George Herbert* 1952.

Allusion

Instead of reading this chapter you might consider the following visual cases of renaissance allusion:

Michelangelo: Sistine Chapel ceiling: relationship of central figures with *ignudi*, prophets, sybils, *putti*.

Raphael: *Parnassus*: relationship of mythological to historical inhabitants.

Poussin: *Lamentation over the dead Christ*: as a parallel to his *Venus with the dead Adonis*.

We cannot share the renaissance habit of allusion. It was a way of proving their position in the map of time; and of proving they were as civilized, or godfearing, as their ancestors. We live in the now. Our imagination reaches towards other worlds which we make as unlike ours as we can, whether we project them into the future or the past. Our sense of time is geared to DEW, orbits, revs – its longest unit is a minute. But the renaissance invented the mechanical clock, and printing; they were living in the past and reproducing it in the present (see McLuhan *Understanding media* ch. 15).

Classical allusion

Even Milton's form is allusive: an epic depends on previous epics; so *PL* both is an allusion to Greek and Latin literature, and contains many allusions to it. It contains actual translations from the classics. The whole of the angels' first battle (VI 207) is like the fight between Zeus and the Titans in Hesiod's *Theogony*; and many details translate classical phrases. When Satan is wounded, 'Forthwith on all sides to his aid was run By angels many and strong' (335): 'was run' = Latin *cursum est*, and the incident imitates the *Iliad* XIV 428–32 where Hector is rescued by his comrades:

> angels many and strong, who interposed
> Defence, while others bore him on their shields
> Back to his chariot; where it stood retired
> From off the files of war; there they him laid
> Gnashing for anguish...

they held their round shields in front of him, and his comrades lifted him in their arms, and bare him out of the battle, till he reached his swift horses that were standing waiting for him, with the charioteer and the fairdight chariot at the rear of the combat and the war. These toward the city bare him heavily moaning.   Lang, Leaf and Myers 1882 rev 1892

Later on, Milton writes of 'where the might of Gabriel fought' (355). In Greek and Latin 'the might of Hercules' = the mighty Hercules. At the end of that day's battle;

> Now night her course began, and over heaven
> Inducing darkness, grateful truce imposed.   406

'Inducing' is odd; it comes from Horace, *iam nox inducere terris umbras. . .parabat.*

But we must not make too much of this. It is there, for readers who know enough Greek and Latin to pick up the paraphrases. But for those who don't, Milton's words are enough. In the first place, there is just as much native English as Greek and Latin. In this part of *PL* Milton uses a lot of medieval words for warfare, such as *broils* (277), *parle* (= parley, 296), *griding* (329), *uncouth* (362), 'the foughten field' (410, as in *Henry V* IV vi 18, 'this glorious and well-foughten field'; it is the Anglo-Saxon past participle). Secondly, the classical paraphrases work as English too. *Inducing* is strange for nightfall, but without knowing Horace we recognize it as a word for the way twilight seems to be drawn across the sky; we hear it rhyming with *truce*; and we notice how the sentence, beginning with the slow inducing of night, is completed with 'grateful truce *imposed*' – quite dark now. 'The might of Gabriel' means 'The mighty Gabriel' in Greek and Latin, but if we forget that, we will read it in Milton's English as something rather different and strange: it is not so much Gabriel himself who is fighting as either Gabriel's angelic might, or, more likely, Gabriel's army. This is a case of Milton using a classical construction to make English flexible, so that it will produce varied rhythms and various meanings.

Biblical allusion

In addition, *PL* being a Christian epic, it depends on the Bible. Christianity is the most literary religion in the world: it is crammed with characters and stories; much of its doctrine was enshrined in poetry – *Job*, the *Psalms*, *Song of Solomon*, *Revelation* – and has been re-enshrined in the liturgy, stained glass, icons, paintings. It is a religion in which the word has a special sanctity. In the 17th century even educated Christians were only just beginning to see that you cannot take the whole Bible literally; its very words still had total authority. Very little of the actual story of *PL* is in the canonical Bible (see section on myth above); but most of the doctrine, and many of the metaphors, are quoted from it:

> Say, heavenly powers, where shall we find such love,
> Which of ye will be mortal to redeem
> Man's mortal crime, and just the unjust to save,
> Dwells in all heaven charity so dear?   III 213

For Christ also hath once suffered for sins, the just for the unjust.
                                                            I Peter iii 18

You can see that allusion may give authority to the objectionable. The epistles of *Peter* are not a good model: paranoiac, vengeful, parochial in space and time. *II Peter* ii attacks heretics and other enemies of the church and prophesies that 'their damnation slumbereth not'. It goes on to cite cases of enemies being damned:

For if God spared not the angels that sinned, but cast them down to hell, and delivered them into chains of darkness, to be reserved unto judgement; and spared not the old world, but saved Noah, the eighth person, a preacher of righteousness, bringing in the flood upon the world of the ungodly...

And the present enemies are treated as animals:

But these, as natural brute beasts, made to be taken and destroyed...shall utterly perish in their own corruption.

That is an invitation to slaughter. Milton took up the image of the abattoir when the Son defeats the rebel angels at the end of VI: 'and as a herd Of goats or timorous flock together thronged Drove them before him thunderstruck'.

Of course there are equally objectionable allusions to the classics. We don't know which has caused more misery – the mother-loving, child-sacrificing, stiff-lipped imperialism that our civilization has at times extracted from Homer and Virgil; or the persecuting self-righteousness drawn from parts of the Bible. The point is that literary allusion can be a lesson in the abuse of authority, as well as in the generous spending of an inheritance. We need an essay on 'The poet as heir'.

Some of the Biblical allusions are richer than they look. The angels' hymn at the end of creation is artificial in form:

> Open, ye everlasting gates, they sung,
> Open, ye heavens, your living doors; let in
> The great Creator from his work returned
> Magnificent, his six days work, a world.   VII 565

But the psalm it quotes enriches, for it is a hymn for the feast of tabernacles, or harvest festival, giving thanks to God as creator:

The earth is the Lord's, and the fulness thereof; the world, and they that dwell therein. For he hath founded it upon the seas, and established it upon the floods...Lift up your heads, O ye gates; and be ye lift up, ye everlasting doors; and the king of glory shall come in. *Ps* xxiv

We may think a Biblical allusion is classical:

> The gray
> Dawn, and the Pléiadès before him danced
> Shedding sweet influence VII 373

Canst thou bind the sweet influence of Pleiades, or loose the band of Orion?
Job xxxviii 31

When this happens it may be because we are not as familiar with the Bible's poetry – the psalms, *Job, Ecclesiastes, Song of Solomon*, parts of *Isaiah* and *Ezekiel* – as we are with its theology. It may also be because we associate 'classical' with marble and laborious correctitude. The cure for that is to look at some pictures of Greek bronzes with the enamel still in their eyes, and the *smaller* Greek works in a museum; and to read the *Greek anthology* and Dodd's *The Greeks and the irrational*. But sometimes Milton himself mixes Biblical and classical references; the result is usually unpleasant. When the Son goes out to destroy the rebel angels he rides in a chariot which Milton takes word for word from visions in *Ezekiel* i and vi and a prayer in *Habakkuk* iii. Then the Son himself is described:

> He in celestial panoply all armed
> Of radiant urim, work divinely wrought,
> Ascended, at his right hand victory
> Sat eagle-winged, beside him hung his bow
> And quiver with three-bolted thunder stored... VI 760

Urim were gems symbolizing judgement between guilt and innocence which the high priest of Israel wore on his chest; but the victory was a small statue of the Greek goddess of victory fixed to the sides of Bronze Age chariots; and although Jehovah occasionally thunders in the Old Testament, the three-pronged thunderbolt is the special attribute of Zeus.

Problems of allusion

When Milton misalludes in that way it is usually, I think, because he is anxious to be specific, to be emphatic, and to get everything in. So his allusions are numerous but tend to be verbal, allusions as it were to the text rather than to what is inside it. There is not much in *PL* of the *feel* of the Bible, or of Homer, anyway as I register it. I miss, for example, the practical details from both sources, the earthenware vessels, soldiers tightening straps, weapons breaking, animals being carefully butchered, sails set. Of course there is no place for them in this poem; but I think Milton ignored them anyway. There isn't much either of the Bible's pastoralism. This is important, as the source of much theological imagery – not only the lambs and wolves, but the whole range of landscape, weather, vegetation. It feeds Herbert's poems directly; but in *PL*, when the Son replaces the shattered hills at the end of the war in heaven,

> At his command the uprooted hills retired
> Each to his place, they heard his voice and went
> Obsequious, heaven his wonted face renewed,
> And with fresh flowerets hill and valley smiled.　　　vi 781

Surely, that wordiness and decor, which are so much of the renaissance, have interposed between us and the Biblical possibilities? In the Bible, God is a god of mountains – 'the foundations also of the hills moved and were shaken, because he was wroth' (*Psalms* xviii 7; cf. xcv the *Venite*; *Job* xxviii; *Nahum* i). In *PL* vi we feel the incident of the mountains to belong rather to epic tradition, and especially to its analogue in Claudian's *Gigantomachia*, rather than the Bible. Again, we miss that wild vitality which nature sometimes shows in the Old Testament – 'the mountains and the hills shall break forth before you into singing, and all the trees of the field shall clap their hands' (*Isaiah* lv 12).

In writing *PL*, Milton was trying to rationalize a myth. So in the details he is exact, and careful to allude to authority in the Bible; but he misses what in the Bible is irrational. For example, he takes many details about the fall of the rebel angels and hell from *Ezekiel* xxxi. That chapter is a gloating prophecy of the fall of Assyria. So we have:

I made the nations to shake at the sound of his fall, when I cast him down to hell with them that descend into the pit.

> Hell heard the insufferable noise, hell saw
> Heaven ruining from heaven and would have fled
> Affrighted; but strict fate had cast too deep
> Her dark foundations, and too fast had bound.　　　*PL* vi 867

But in hell we have nothing so desolately ghastly as this:

And strangers, the terrible of the nations, have cut him off, and have left him: upon the mountains and in all the valleys his branches are fallen, and his boughs are broken by all the rivers of the land; and all the people of the earth are gone down from his shadow, and have left him. Upon his rain shall all the fowls of the heaven remain, and all the beasts of the field shall be upon his branches. . . *Ez* xxxi 12

There is very little *sinister* in *PL*; and little of its complement, the thrilling, or its opposite the friendly. We can't have everything. At its worst rationalism can lead, in politics and at home as well as in poetry, to a famished rigour; but at its best it supports the normal; in depriving us of thrills it also protects us from superstition, anarchy – whatever are the worsts on the other side.

We shall never be as familiar with the Bible and the classics as Milton, and the first few generations of his readers, were. Even for them, some of the allusions would be obscure: every schoolboy might recognize the devils' games in Book II as an allusion to the *Iliad* xxii and the *Aeneid* v, and even 'shun the goal With rapid wheels' as a translation of *metaque fervidis evitata rotis* from Horace's first ode; but who would recognize 'Amram's son' (I 339)? It is both classical and Biblical – not merely an allusion to Moses, but an attempt to name him in classical style, as Aeneas is addressed *Anchisa generate*, offspring of Anchises. There is no point in learning about Amram – he is mentioned only three times in the Bible, in genealogical tables which nobody reads; the point is to understand what Milton was doing. Another periphrasis for Moses is richer: 'That shepherd, who first taught the chosen seed' (I 8) links him with the Good Shepherd; it asserts that unity of the Old and New Testaments as a revelation of God's will. That revelation is what classical literature lacks.

Quite often, what we treat as allusion is plain instruction or reminder, as in a sermon:

> Next Chemos, th'óbscene dread of Moab's sons,
> From Aroer to Nebo, and the wild
> Of southmost Abarim; in Hesebon
> And Horonaim, Seon's realm, beyond
> The flowery dale of Sibma clad with vines,
> And Eleálè to the asphaltic pool.   I 406

At one level, Milton is trying to match Greek poetry and legend with English poetry and Hebrew legend. He is emulating the catalogue of troops in the *Iliad* II:

The citizens of Argos and Tiryns of the Great Walls; the men of Hermione and Asine, towns that embrace a deep gulf of the sea; and those from Troezen, from Eionae, and from vine-clad Epidaurus, with the Archaean youth of Aegin and Moses, were led by Diomedes of the loud war-cry. . .

trans. RIEU, Penguin

But Milton cannot match Homer out of the Bible: 'The flowery dale of Sibma' can never be to England what 'vine-clad Epidaurus' is to Greece. Hence the didactic quality of Milton's verse: he has to force his English readers to recollect *Jeremiah* xlviii where Moab is cursed:

From the cry of Heshbon even unto Elealeh, and even unto Jahaz, have they uttered their voice, from Zoar even unto Horonaim...Woe be unto thee, O Moab! the people of Chemosh perisheth...   34...46

With this, the 'allusion' becomes very complicated. The first level is literary, purely aesthetic, and imitative of Homer; the second is didactic, reminding the audience of Hebrew history and geography; the final level is moral, turning the Homeric glory into Jeremiah's curse: the fallen angels' heroism is anathema.

This third level is more important than the first and second. In some ways it is easier to grasp: you need to have read and taken the feeling of the first few chapters of *Genesis, I* and *II Kings, Job*, some of the *Psalms*, some of *Isaiah* and some of *Revelation*. The second level, of factual detail – the fact that Nebo is part of the range of Abarim – is of little literary significance. Look at a map, as Milton did. The first level, of mere allusion, is the most difficult: it will work fully only if you know the originals, especially the classical originals, by heart. The best alternative to that is to read translations of:

Homer *Iliad* I–II: invocation: council of gods: council of war.
   Odyssey IX–XII: voyage: underworld: Circe etc. The most attractive translation at present is by Robert Fitzgerald 1962.
Virgil *Aeneid* I and VI: gods and men: underworld. See also K. W. Gransden *PL* and the *Aeneid* in *Essays in criticism* XVII 1967.
Ovid *Metamorphoses* I: chaos: creation: flood; V: Helicon and Muses: Ceres and Persephone; X–XI: Orpheus and Eurydice. Use the translation by Horace Gregory in Mentor Books, originally Viking 1958.

Language

Vocabulary

The core vocabulary that people keep up for everyday use in advanced societies is about 10,000 words, whatever the language. A highly educated person may have 100,000 words available to him; but it is possible to live on about 600 of modern English. Shakespeare used 15,000 in his writing. Milton used about 8,000 for his poetry; his prose must raise the total to at least 15,000.

Idiomatic diction

Milton's poetic language feels alien. It would surprise most readers that *PL* contains such words and phrases as these:

where he fell flat	I 461
sets them all agape	V 357
No fear lest dinner cool...so down they sat And to their viands fell	V 396...433
mangled	VI 368
sewers...dairy	IX 446...451
Down a while He sat	X 457
spattering noise	X 567
Smote him into the midriff with a stone	XI 445
from bad to worse	XII 106
O that men (Canst thou believe?) should be so stupid grown	XII 115
botches and blanes	XII 180
Be sure they will, said the angel	XII 485

This idiomatic language occurs mostly in three contexts. One is satire, usually against the fallen angels (or the sinful humans they may represent), as at I 461, X 567; or the folly of men, especially intellectual folly as at V 357 and in the Limbo of Fools, where Roman catholic documents 'upwhirled aloft Fly o'er the backside of the world' (III 493). The second is when human and spiritual meet. Here Milton uses everyday language to emphasize the reality of angels, so we have 'No fear lest dinner cool' at V 396. The same thing tends to happen, for the same reason, in metaphysical poems and sermons. The third context is the world after the fall.

Flat everyday idioms are frequent in *PR* and *SA*: 'Close in a cottage low together got' (*PR* I 27), 'here and there' (III 263), 'just in time' (III 298), 'avoided as a blab' (*SA* 495); and they are a major element in Milton's prose. There, his latent metaphorical power is fully expressed in anger and scorn:

And it is still episcopacy that before all our eyes worsens and slugs the most learned and seeming-religious of our ministers; who no sooner advanced to it but, like a seething pot set to cool, sensibly exhale and reek out the greater part of that zeal and those gifts which were formerly in them, settling in a skinny congealment of ease and sloth at the top; and if they keep their learning by some potent sway of nature it is a rare chance; but their devotion most commonly comes to that queasy temper of lukewarmness that gives a vomit to God himself.   *Of reformation*

It is often anger and contempt that made him write so naturally – hence the fluency of Satan's speeches and the boisterous scorn for Roman catholics in the Limbo of Fools, and for hireling priests in *Lycidas*. It is not a happy gift. Even his arguments for love, and freedom from unloving bondage, in *The doctrine and discipline of divorce*, keep falling into angry emphasis:

and with all generous persons thus it is, that where the mind and person please aptly, there some unaccomplishment of the body's delight may be better borne with, than when the mind hangs off in an unclosing disproportion, though the body be as it ought; for there all corporeal delight will soon become unsavoury and contemptible. . .such a marriage can be no marriage where the most honest end is wanting; and the aggrieved person shall do more manly to be extraordinary and singular in claiming the due right whereof he is frustrated than to piece up his lost contentment by visiting the stews or stepping to his neighbour's bed (which is the common shift in this misfortune) or else by suffering his useful life to waste away and be lost under a secret affliction of an unconscionable size to human strength.

There seem to be too many words there.

Milton's simplest language is in the comments he makes on himself and in his own voice. His tone then is purified of derision and of pride:

> unless an age too late, or cold
> Climate, or years damp my intended wing
> Depressed, as much they may, if all be mine,
> Not hers [the Muse's] who brings it nightly to my ear   IX 44

> For still they knew, and ought to have still remembered
> The high injunction not to taste that fruit,
> Whoever tempted.   X 12

Mixed diction

This sort of Miltonic language seems unfamiliar because it tends to be overcome by the grander style of the epic as a whole. When Satan returns to hell after the fall, he meets Sin and Death coming the other way to invade the universe. He directs them to the earth:

> You two this way, among those numerous orbs
> All yours, right down to paradise descend   X 397

'Those numerous orbs' reassert the epic style.

That style is of course predominant. We register its vocabulary as being above our heads, abnormally abstract. Actually, it is probably the clash between abstract and concrete, or learned and idiomatic, that makes us uncomfortable – or the sense of a gap between them. Here is a passage from *Samson* that can be polarized in this way:

	But what availed this temperance, not complete	availed temperance
	Against another object more enticing?	object enticing
what boots it	What boots it at one gate to make defence	defence
let in	And at another to let in the foe	
	Effeminately vanquished? by which means,	effeminately vanquished
blind shamed etc....	Now blind, disheartened, shamed, dishonoured, quelled,	disheartened etc....
	To what can I be useful, wherein serve	
	My nation, and the work from heaven imposed,	
	But to sit idle on the household hearth,	
	A burdenous drone...etc.	

If you complete the analysis to the end of the speech at 577, how does each column register separately, just as a list of words? What effect do they have on one another when put together in sentences and lines?

Learned diction

Some of the strangeness of Milton's words is not his but his epoch's. We blame it on him because we don't read the others. They could write like this:

But I am over-tedious in these toys, which, howsoever in some men's too severe censures, they may be held absurd and ridiculous, I am the bolder to insert, as not borrowed from circumforanean rogues and gypsies but out of the writings of worthy philosophers and physicians (yet living some of them) and religious professors in famous universities, who are able to patronise that which they have said, and vindicate themselves from all cavillers and ignorant persons.

ROBERT BURTON after 'A digression of spirits and witchcraft' in
Anatomy of melancholy I ii l IV 1621

These [angels] are certainly the magisterial and masterpieces of the Creator, the flower, or (as we may say) the best part of nothing; actually existing, what we are but in hopes and probability. We are only that amphibious piece between a corporal and spiritual essence, that middle form that links those two together, and makes good the method of God and nature, that jumps not from extremes, but unites the incompatible distances by some middle and participating natures. That we are the breath and similitude of God, it is indisputable, and upon record of holy scripture; but to call ourselves a microcosm, or little world, I thought it only a pleasant trope of rhetoric, till my near judgement and second thoughts told me there was a real truth therein. For first we are a rude mass, and in the rank of creatures which only are, and have a dull kind of being, not yet privileged with life or preferred to sense or reason; next we live the life of plants, the life of animals, the life of men, and at last the life of spirits, running on in one mysterious nature those five kinds of existences, which comprehend the creatures not only of the world but of the universe. Thus is man that great and true amphibian, whose nature is disposed to live, not only like other creatures in divers elements, but in divided and distinguished worlds: for though there be but one to sense, there are two to reason, the one visible, the other invisible; whereof Moses seems to have left description, and of the other so obscurely, that some parts thereof are yet in controversy. And truly, for the first chapters of Genesis, I must confess a great deal of obscurity; though divines have to the power of human reason endeavoured to make all go in a literal meaning, yet those allegorical interpretations are also probable, and perhaps the mystical method of Moses bred up in the hieroglyphical schools of the Egyptians.

SIR THOMAS BROWNE *Religio medici* 1642

Might souls converse with souls by angel-way,
Enfranchised from their prisoning clay,
What strains, by intuition, would they then convey!

But spirits sublimed too fast evaporate may
Without some interposed allay;
And notions subtilised too thin exhale away.

EDWARD BENLOWES *Theophila or love's sacrifice* Canto i 1652

All qualities ran wildly up and down
Ne'er thinking of symbolic amity;
All motions were transverse; as yet unknown
Were rest and quiet; hideous ataxy
Was everything; and neither here nor there
    Keeped their own homes, but all were everywhere.

PROFESSOR JOSEPH BEAUMONT on the creation in
Psyche or love's mystery Canto vi 1648

It is true that Burton and Browne were bachelor scholars; Burton was a suicidal depressive and Browne, as he admits, 'austere, my behaviour full of rigour, sometimes not without morosity'. Benlowes was an amateur scholar; Beaumont was a professor of divinity and master of Peterhouse. This suggests quite a lot about the psychopathology of learned diction: it does seem to be a symptom of the anal temperament, of the need to hoard things that somehow symbolize what could have been a love-gift – the child retaining its faeces, Burton's endless quotations, Browne's scientific collections, Benlowes's years in the Bodleian Library.

But symptoms of this kind are shaped by the environment as well; in some cases perhaps the individual may as it were suffer a pathological condition on behalf of society. During the first half of the 17th century, writers crammed the far-fetched in. They were trying to handle increasing inputs of information from more and more different sources – the Bible, classical poetry, Plato's philosophy, Aristotle's philosophy, history, modern science. Any one bit of this information was likely to be packed with latent references to other things, because of the many sources of input. This supplied the lyric poet, or the wit, with automatic metaphor. You had only to think of a phoenix and you had a Greek bird that lived in Arabia, where the spices came from; it had been described in colourful detail by classical writers, and in Anglo-Saxon, and had by now appeared in many modern works; it was an emblem of fire, lovers, Christ, death, resurrection, immortality, chastity. But for the prose-writer or the epic poet – a writer trying to organize and retail coherent information on a large scale – for him it presented an enormous problem of storage and output. Among the methods of handling, allusion, syntax and diction were crucial: allusion as a signpost or shortcut; syntax as the carrier; and a diction in which abstracts were especially valuable because they can contain several ideas at once.

Here are some of the learned words in *PL* which look Miltonic but were actually already in use by other writers. Some of them date from the middle ages; most come from the great word-making phase of the 16th century; a few – the dated ones – were recent (the dates being the Oxford dictionary's for the first recorded use).

alimental	V 424	innumerous	VII 455
atrophy 1620	XI 486	irriguous	IV 255
attrite 1625	X 1073	jaculation 1608	VI 665
cincture	IX 1117	lucent	III 589
conflagrant	XII 548	nocent	IX 186
congratulant	X 458	pendulous 1605	IV 1000
debel	IV 605	plenipotent 1658	X 404
exorbitant	III 177	procinct	VI 19
fusil	XI 573	sciential	IX 837
hyaline 1661	VII 619	stupendous 1666	X 351
illaudable	VI 382	succinct	III 643
implicit	VII 323		

Those are also examples of words that Milton used only once in *PL*. He did that with an abnormally high proportion of his total vocabulary. No doubt the habit contributes much to the sense of strangeness; for a writer can acclimatize strange words by frequent use. Some of his once-only words look odd for another reason, that though used by others they did not survive. They were unnecessary, or beaten by another version: *innumerous* by *innumerable* (which he also used), *illaudable* by *unpraiseworthy*. It was a matter of evolutionary luck, which words you chose and which survived of all the words that had been imported from French or coined from Greek or Latin in the 16th century.

Milton and Shakespeare

Many of Shakespeare's choices were discarded – *continuate* (*Timon* I i), *intrinsicate* (*Antony* v ii), *undividable* (*Errors* II ii). But with Shakespeare we are more conscious of unique words, words he seems to have made up for himself in the heat of the moment, to articulate a single idea:

> dispropertied *Coriolanus* III i
> immoment *Antony* v ii
> imperceiverant *Cymbeline* IV i
> incarnadine *Macbeth* II ii

Milton invented very few words – perhaps *displode* (= explode VI 605) *loquacious* (x 161) *omnific* (VII 217) *serried* (I 548, VI 599). He was not trying to represent highly individuated ideas and feelings so much as general ones, so he did not need to invent; and for epic he could write more slowly than for drama, and choose his words deliberately. That is why they are sometimes oppressive: they are meant literally, instead of as quick expressions of feeling; we have to take them seriously; and when Milton chooses wrongly, it matters more than when Shakespeare does.

Shakespeare used words to express; Milton, to define. *Omnific* is not a word that 'came to him', as *discandy* (*Antony* IV xii) must have come to Shakespeare; it comes *from* the Latin *omnis+ficus* = all-making. In the context, of course, it is effective; even out of context, *petrific* works (x 294). But Milton's language, and its context, are artificial compared with Shakespeare's, so we cannot so often understand his words by intuition; they demand conscious translation.

Because this is so, we ought not to worry too much – the profit may be small, and restricted to the context of *PL*. For example, in Book x the angels sing to God:

> Just are thy ways,
> Righteous are thy decrees on all thy works;
> Who can extenuate thee?

This is puzzling: *extenuate* refers to things that might make one seem less guilty; Milton uses it that way in *Samson*: 'not that I endeavour To lessen or extenuate my offence', (767). But how could God need to be extenuated? The word comes from the Latin *extenuare*, to make thin; and in the 17th century it could mean this in several ways, of which the thinning of guilt was only one; until the end of the 18th century it could mean what it means here, to lessen, weaken, slight. Shakespeare used it in both senses:

> thus to persist
> In doing wrong extenuates not wrong,
> But makes it much more heavy.　　　　　*Troilus* II ii

> Cleopatra, know,
> We will extenuate rather than enforce.　　*Antony* v ii

But in the second, rarer, use, Shakespeare's context helps – as, on a larger scale, the context of melt-ing words in *Antony* helps to explain the invented word *discandy*. Milton's context does not help. The word cannot be explained by reference to the angels' feelings or our own experience. Its meaning lies in itself alone; to understand it, we must know the word. But the word in that sense is dead; and Milton has not given it life, as some poets give life to learned words:

> sheer plod makes plough down *sillion*
> Shine...　　　　　　　　　　　Hopkins *Windhover*

> Flesh fade, and mortal trash
> Fall to the *residuary* worm...　　　　*Heraclitean fire*

Milton's invention *gurge* is a fitting word for a whirlpool (XII 41) but he made it by thinking about the Latin *gurges* rather than about whirlpools: it is a word-word, not a thing-word.

Language and philosophy

For our own survival, we are bound to resist the word-word. We are likely to feel what Edwin Muir said about it in a poem on Calvinist kirks called *The incarnate one* (1956):

> The Word made flesh is here made word again,
> A word made word in flourish and arrogant crook.
> See there King Calvin with his iron pen,
> And God three angry letters in a book,

And there the logical hook
On which the Mystery is impaled and bent
Into an ideological instrument.
There's better gospel in man's natural tongue

. . . .

The fleshless word, growing, will bring us down,
Pagan and Christian man alike will fall,
The auguries say, the white and black and brown,
The merry and sad, theorist, lover, all
Invisibly will fall:
Abstract calamity, save for those who can
Build their cold empire on the abstract man.

Roy Fuller's *Perturbations of Uranus* carries the same message. Yet in Milton's time it may have seemed otherwise. The great enemy was not a computer programmed to annihilation. They believed in a power above the doomsday machine: grace pre-empts the last judgement. The enemies were more gross and new – blind mouths, persecution, arbitrary taxation. The freedoms we have owe something to the play of Milton's mind on abstractions such as liberty, justice, toleration.

Those two ways of using language imply two philosophies related to knowledge and behaviour. Milton's way, of word-words, assumes that words invoke ultimate realities which are imperceivable by the senses but do actually in some sort exist. It is a Platonic philosophy; or a philosophy of innate ideas. It assumes the concept HORSE somewhere really exists; or is embedded in our brains: and that concept is of true and perfect horseness. The actual horses that we see with our senses are imperfect manifestations of HORSE. In this philosophy, energy flows from the mind onto experience; sensory experience is regarded as less reliable than mental, and subjugated to it. Paradoxically, it is called a 'realist' kind of philosophy, because it thinks of HORSE as the true reality.

Thing-words such as Shakespeare used assume a different philosophy, in which sensation produces concepts by practice and teaching: we have an idea of horseness from seeing a lot of horses.

The original of them all [thoughts] is that which we call 'sense', for there is no conception in a man's mind that hath not at first, totally or by parts, been begotten upon the organs of sense. The rest are derived from that original.   HOBBES *Leviathan* ch. 1 1651

The steps by which the mind attains several truths: The senses at first let in particular ideas, and furnish the yet empty cabinet; and the mind by degrees growing familiar with some of them, they are lodged in the memory, and names got to them. Afterwards, the mind proceeding further, abstracts

114

them, and by degrees learns the use of general names. In this manner, the mind comes to be furnished with ideas and language, the materials about which to exercise its discursive faculty; and the use of reason becomes daily more visible, and these materials that give it employment increase. But though the having of general ideas and the use of general words and reason usually grow together, yet I see not how this any way proves them innate.   JOHN LOCKE *Essay concerning human understanding* ch. 2 1690

This is on the empirical or nominalist side – empirical because based on experience; nominalist because you don't think of H O R S E as existing independently of horses – it is just a name for your experience of horses.

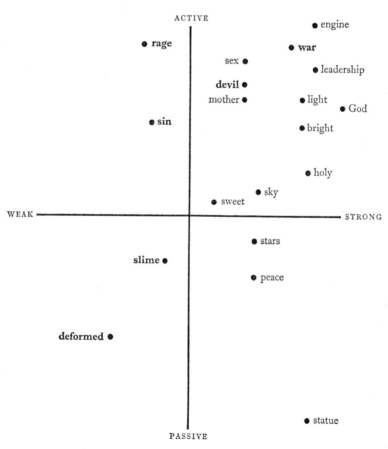

(Disapproved concepts are shown in bold type.)

If you belong to the first school, you are likely to be fairly sure of the difference between right and wrong. As Descartes put it:

since God has endowed each of us with some light of reason by which to distinguish truth from error. . .all that is necessary to right action is right judgement, and to the best action the most correct judgement.

Discourse on method pt 3 1637

On the other hand, if you belong to the second school you will tend to see morals as relative and subjective, like Hobbes:

these words of good, evil, and contemptible, are ever used with relation to the person that useth them, there being nothing simply and absolutely so.

ch. 6

You can see the problem of good versus evil in *PL* by looking at the position of words in what is called a semantic differential space. The figure on p. 115 shows roughly where a few of the relevant words lie, on the basis of subjects tested by J. J. Jenkins *et al.* for their *Atlas of semantic profiles for 360 words* in the *American Journal of Psychology* 71 (1958) 688–99.

Latin

Original writers use difficult words. T. S. Eliot has *anfractuous, appetency, barbituric, periphrastic, sempiternal*; or consider Wallace Stevens. But they are obviously using difficult words *because* they are difficult, for special purposes. This is often so with Milton's difficult diction, his Latin words. If we started learning Latin before about 1970, its reputation may be as evil as inorganic chemistry's. In the 17th century its influence was not only stronger than it is now but felt much more naturally, like the Roman urns that decorate the parapets of Jacobean buildings, or the Roman torsos carved on the organ screen in King's chapel, Cambridge. What's more, Latin was felt to be a language not merely (as we perhaps feel it) of war, law and theology, but of nature, luxury and love (Lucretius, Ovid, Catullus). It was also the language of newness, a way of saying things not said before in English.

Milton's latinisms have a ponderous philosophical air:

oblivious	I 266
omnific	VII 217
participate	VIII 390
pernicious	I 282
prevenient	XI 3
unobnoxious	VI 404
unsucceeded	V 821

Many quite comfortable words are polysyllabic; these are uncomfortable because they are made up largely of prefixes and suffixes and grammatical endings.

Science

Foreign words feel at home in English when they are names for things or ideas in daily use, like some of our recent scientific borrowings – *atom, electricity, gene, nitrous* (*PL* IV 815, VI 512), *nuclear, polythene*; and when we have learnt to shorten them – *bus*. A lot of Milton's Latin words were in the 17th century not much less familiar as scientific terms than those are now, especially the astronomical ones:

eccentric	III 575, V 623, VIII 83
ecliptic	III 740
epicycle	VIII 84
equinoctial	II 637, IX 64, X 672
ethereal	26 times in *PL*
lateral	X 705
nocturnal and	
diurnal rhomb	VIII 134
optic tube	I 288, III 590
sideral	IX 693
telescope	IV 42

And there are more organic words such as *embryon* (II 900, VII 277), 'alimental recompense in humid exhalation' (V 425), *naphtha* (I 729). But not only have the 'facts' of science changed, so has the familiarity of different sciences. In the 17th century, especially in poems taking a cosmic view, the emphasis was on astronomy, meteorology, optics, where now it is on molecular structure; even space physics is mostly discussed in terms of electronic engineering.

Double meanings

What is really peculiar about Milton's English, though, is his use of latinate words in their Latin sense. Other 17th-century writers did this, but it is an idiosyncrasy. In most cases both the original Latin and the modified English senses were available; but Milton deliberately uses both at once, or only the Latin. In either case he forces you to recollect the Latin and so introduce a conscious act of construing into your response:

abject fallen angels = miserable, and thrown down, *abiectus* I 312; but
  just miserable at IX 572.
complicated snakes = twisted together, *complicatus* X 523.

conspicuous universe = visible VII 63.
disastrous eclipse = astronomically ominous – *aster*, star I 597.
erroneous poet = wandering, *erroneus* VII 20.
fervid wheels = red-hot, *fervidis* VII 224.
frequent seats = crowded, *frequens* I 797.
in procinct = stood to arms, *in procinctu* VI 19.
night *invests* the sea = wraps, *investire* I 208.
involved in smoke = wrapped or wreathed in, *involvere* I 236.
incumbent on the air = leaning, *incumbens* I 226.
inhabit lax = take your ease, and/or spread out, *habitare laxe* VII 162.
punctual spot = small as a point, *punctum* VIII 23.
reluctant = struggling to and fro, *luctantis* VI 58 X 515 1045.
succinct tunic = girt up, ready, *succingere, succinctus* III 643.
voluble snake = rolling, *volubilis* IX 436.

This is all a kind of play. Sometimes it is learned punning: 'that small infantry' (I 575) = warlike pygmies, little people like infants. In *PL* VI, where it is rampant, Milton is parodying military epic – 'incentive reed' (519) = match; *jaculation* = hurling, *iaculatio* (665).

Even so, in the last resort we may disapprove of this use of language if the people we know in real life who speak with deliberate pedantry do so for sad reasons. It is sometimes a way of asserting superiority, or keeping us at a distance, this insistent learned flippancy. But there are people who use such language seriously, not to be pedantic or funny but to be accurate or rapid. We judge it by the occasion: no-one thinks less of an article in *Nature* or *Mind* for using technical shorthand. In *PL* a rough test is, is this pedantic word necessary in the context? If not, does its quality – strangeness, sound, rhythm – help us? *Increate* in the theological context of III 6 might be excused on the first count, *incumbent* of Satan flying through smoke on the second; but 'Meanwhile inhabit lax, ye powers of heaven' seems a profitless attempt to copy the letter of Latin. Even that, of course, we may approve if we understand it. Language like

> from one entire globose
> Stretched into longitude   V 750

> all heaven,
> And happy constellations on that hour
> Shed their selectest influence   VIII 511

has an eccentric energy not to be despised. At its most eccentric it does not suggest powers of mind or feeling that would make for a happy or efficient life; but this after all is not a person talking, but a poem.

It is ironical that Milton's poetry has become a textbook for grammarians' footnotes, for he wrote it as a revolution in language.

The 18th century enjoyed Milton all the more for seeing how odd he is: 'very Elegant and New, and full of Energy' the Richardsons said of IX 401.

Romance

Latin preponderates, but Milton drew words from other cultures as well. There is a class of 'romantic' words. Some are derived from oriental languages via the crusades:

caravan	VII 428
divan	X 457
panim = pagan	X 765
soldan = sultan	I 764

Others from Italian:

ammiral	I 294
brown = dark, like *bruno* in Italian poetry	IX 1088
sdein as in Spenser = disdain	IV 50
serenate	IV 769
vans = wings	II 927

And French, the language of chivalry:

career = joust	I 766
champain = plain of battle	VI 2
seneshal = steward	IX 38

Milton uses this class of words in military contexts, usually with a note of disdain or parody.

Pastoral

Even the rural English dialect that Milton sometimes uses seems to come from Spenser, or to be part of a pastoral convention, instead of representing natural speech:

draff = rubbish	X 630
frore = freezing	II 595
grunsel = threshold	I 460
tine = kindle	X 1075
yeanling = newborn animal	III 434

But this is because, like all renaissance writers, Milton had a strong sense of decorum. In a pastoral passage you might use country language, but you would not use it like a countryman because you were still in control, writing an epic. So when Satan comes to tempt

Eve like a town cad bringing his corruption into the country, there are country-words (e.g. *kine*) and town-words (*sewers*) but the whole is formal still. Milton-words (*populous*) prevail:

> As one who long in populous city pent,
> Where houses thick and sewers annoy the air,
> Forth issuing on a summer's morn to breathe
> Among the pleasant villages and farms
> Adjoined, from each thing met conceives delight,
> The smell of grain, or tedded grass [tossed for hay], or kine,
> Or dairy, each rural sight, each rural sound... IX 445

At XII 634, Michael is showing Adam the future so fast that Milton exercises several different styles in 50 lines. There is war – 'Giants of mighty bone, and bold emprise'; pastoral – 'A herd of beeves, fair oxen and fair kine From a fat meadow ground; or fleecy flock, Ewes and their bleating lambs'; politics – 'harangues are heard, but soon In factious opposition'; and moralizing – 'so violence Proceeded, and oppression, and sword-law'. Each passage has its own diction, within Milton's style.

Grand style

Milton's grander diction was so much imitated in the 18th century, and by the Romantics (there are several quotations from him in *Tintern Abbey*) that it has come to look derivative itself. In fact, many of his 'Miltonisms' were, when he used them, fresh; others were colloquial; but there is an overriding weight – what Dr Johnson called 'gigantic loftiness' – which may oppress us if the meaning is not dense enough to support it. For example:

> the sulphurous hail
> Shot after us in storm, o'erblown hath laid
> The fiery surge, that from the precipice
> Of heaven received us falling, and the thunder,
> Winged with red lightning and impetuous rage,
> Perhaps hath spent his shafts, and ceases now
> To bellow through the vast and boundless deep... I 171

As the passage goes on, it is the quantity of words that oppresses, rather than anything peculiar about them. Indeed, though distinct enough one by one, they coagulate into uniformity. Each unit of meaning – fieriness, largeness, noisiness – is given so many stresses that instead of being faceted (different kinds of fieriness) it becomes stodgy (one general lump of fieriness). Thus, we have:

FIRE	sulphurous fiery red etc.
STORM	hail storm o'erblown etc.
ATTACK	shot falling impetuous etc.

On the other hand:

Milton's grandeur and his subtlety (my concern in the next chapter) often co-exist in the very same lines, which makes it particularly important not to cordon off the poem from meddling practical critics. The following lines would generally be agreed to belong to Milton's sterner style, but their bareness is combined with local subtlety to produce an effect of astonishing breadth and power:

> So glister'd the dire Snake, and into fraud
> Led Eve our credulous Mother, to the Tree
> Of prohibition, root of all our woe.   IX 643–5

These lines stamp themselves at once as in the Grand Style. What is remarkable, though, is that they are verbally subtle and active without any fussiness or any blurring of the grand austerity. I am thinking not only of the sombre gleam in the pun on *root*; but also of subtler effects: the playing of the bright *glister* against the dark *dire*, for instance. Or the superb use of the curt 'snake'... CHRISTOPHER RICKS *Milton's grand style* 1963

Materials

Here is a short selection of words that Milton used in a sense different from ours:

admire	I 690, VIII 25 75	marble	III 564
advise	II 42 376, V 729, IX 212	nice	IV 241, V 433, VI 584,
amiable	IV 250, VIII 484, IX 899		VIII 399
buxom	II 842, V 270	pomp	VII 564, VIII 61
decent	III 644	prevent	II 739, IV 996, X 987, XI 3
enormous	I 511, V 297, VII 411	sad	V 94, V 564
exorbitant	III 177	satiate	VII 282, VIII 214
explode	X 546, XI 669	secure	XI 746
fame	I 651, II 346, IV 938, X 481	virtue	I 320, II 483, III 586,
intend	II 457		IV 671, V 371, VIII 124
lawn	IV 252		etc.
manure	IV 628, XI 28		

Here are a few words used by Milton and/or Shakespeare with special poetic effect. Context and meaning can be checked in concordances to Milton and Shakespeare and in the *Shorter Oxford dictionary*:

bland	nitrous	permissive
complacent	obnoxious	rare
florid	obsequious	visual
heinous	opacous	voluminous
inexorably	participate	

Syntax

More than Milton's diction, it is his syntax that puzzles. In the passage analysed for diction in the section above, the kernel of the first sentence is 'The hail hath laid the surge'. But the hail and surge, in addition to being sulphurous and fiery, are heavily qualified by clauses that come after them, as in Latin, so that the mind has to double back on the sequence. It is the hail which *was* 'shot after us in storm' and now *is* 'o'erblown'; the surge is that which received us *when we were falling* from the precipice of heaven.

This kind of syntax is called in linguistics 'self-embedding', in contrast to 'branching', e.g.

branching	When it rained, the fire went out
	The fire went out when it rained
self-embedding	The fire, when it rained, went out

The self-embedding type feels less natural; yet it is closest to the causal sequence fire–rain–out. The branching types are less logical: rain–fire–out; fire–out–rain; but we grasp them as sense-wholes, rather than logical sequences, and as wholes they make sense. The self-embedding type is difficult to grasp as a whole; it is designed to be followed in bits, as a sequence; but if the middle bits are long and complicated, we may very well have forgotten, when we get to the end – that is, to the event, the result – what the causal beginning was. That sometimes happens when we read Milton.

Participles and Latinism

The self-embedding type of writing ties its complications into the middle with conjunctions and prepositions, and with participles. Milton uses a lot of both. His participles are a source of difficulty for most readers. The *shot, o'erblown* and *falling* of that passage above are not too bad; but in the one below there are a great many, and all are based on past participles as used in Latin:

He *after Eve seduced, unminded* slunk	X 332
Into the wood fast by, and changing shape	
To observe the sequel, saw his guileful act	
By Eve, though all unweeting, *seconded*	335
Upon her husband, saw their shame that sought	
Vain covertures; but when he saw descend	
The Son of God to judge them, *terrified*	

He fled, not hoping to escape, but shun
The present, fearing guilty what his wrath   340
Might suddenly inflict; *that past*, returned
By night, and listening where the hapless pair
Sat in their sad discourse, and various plaint,
Thence gathered his own doom, which understood
Not instant, but of future time. With joy   345
And tidings *fraught*, to hell he now returned,
And at the brink of chaos, near the foot
Of this new wondrous pontifice, *unhoped*
Met who to meet him came, his offspring dear.

Grammatical name	Latin	English
present infinitive	corrumpere	to seduce
past participle passive (feminine)	corrupta	(having been) seduced
past participle passive used as an adjective	Eva corrupta	seduced Eve, Eve-who-had been-seduced
past participle passive with *post* (or *ante*)+ accusative	post Evam corruptam	after Eve had been seduced
past participle passive with ablative, i.e. ablative absolute	Eva corrupta, Satanus fugit	Eve having been seduced, Satan fled

If you don't know Latin, take no notice of that. The important points
are that these are all ways of writing about the past; and they are
ways of writing about things that have been done to people, i.e.
passive. They don't translate into ordinary English, as you can see
from the right-hand column, but Milton uses them in the passage
above, precisely for their past and passive qualities. In addition to the
italicized constructions, 'With joy And tidings' is a classical way of
saying joyful tidings; and 'Met who to meet him came' is Latin in its
reliance on inflected pronouns. The passage is made more difficult by
the extreme density of its pastness, active as well as passive – *slunk*,
sought, *fled* etc; by the present participles operating inside this
pastness – *changing*, *fearing*, *listening*; and by the crushing together of
parts of speech as in 'but shun The present, fearing guilty' at 340 =
but hoping to shun the present wrath, fearing it because he was guilty.

This passage is so extraordinary that we must assume Milton was
experimenting. He was moving several characters about the cosmos
at once and quickly. Latin does that sort of thing well: its literature is
often concerned with the unwieldy but disciplined movement of
troops and concepts round an empire. Unfortunately in English the
economy is lost in our discomfort; the words jostle and the syntax
clogs the action it is meant to speed. (What way of life does our sort
of language imply?)

Ellipsis

A further difficulty of Milton's syntax is caused, as in Shakespeare and Hopkins, by abbreviation or 'ellipsis'. He often omits pronouns, articles, *of*, the verb *to be*, etc. E.g. 'Peace is despaired, For who can think [of] submission?' (I 660); 'yet no purposed foe To you whom I could pity thus forlorn Though I [am] unpitied' (IV 373); 'To find [one] who might direct his wandering flight' (III 631); Satan turned into a snake, 'punished in the shape [in which] he sinned' (x 516). Often these abbreviations are Latinisms: 'those rebellious' (I 71) = *eis rebellantibus*; 'as they sat recline' (IV 333) uses the Latin adjective *reclinis*.

Impressionistic syntax

It is best to think of these habits not in terms of grammar or Latin, but as tending experimentally towards impressionistic syntax: at times, almost its abolition. When Adam is telling the story of his creation he says that after finding himself alive, as if woken from sleep, he lay down and really went to sleep:

> there gentle sleep
> First found me, and with soft oppression seized
> My drowsèd sense, untroubled, though I thought
> I then was passing to my former state
> Insensible, and forthwith to dissolve.   VIII 287

'Forthwith to dissolve' has not much authority even in Latin; it is a sleepy version of 'was forthwith to dissolve'. Similarly when Satan at the gates of hell looks out into chaos:

> Into this wild abyss the wary fiend
> Stood on the brink of hell and looked a while,
> Pondering his voyage   II 917

There is no point in claiming that, because you can't 'stand into', *stood* is a past participle passive used as an adjective; the point is simply that Milton is fusing the notions of standing and looking, to give the sense of vertigo.

Here is Satan standing on the outside globe of the universe, looking down at God's creation:

> Such wonder seized, though after heaven seen,
> The spirit malign, but much more envy seized
> At sight of all this world beheld so fair...   III 552

The syntax presents: wonder – flashback to heaven – flash forward to malignity – malignity converts wonder to envy – the universe spread out beneath that envy.

Then he flies down through the universe towards the earth:

> and winds with ease
> Through the pure marble art his óblique way
> Amongst innumerable stars, that shone
> Stars distant, but nigh hand seemed other worlds
> Or other worlds they seemed, or happy isles
> Like those Hesperian Gardens famed of old...

'That shone / Stars distant' = that shone as stars from a distance... but, close to, looked like other worlds. The abbreviation, working with the pause at the end of the line, enacts the distant shining. The stars he passes fluctuate in distance like film shots.

Milton's impressionistic syntax can be poignant. This is the garden of Eden:

> Thus was this place,
> A happy rural seat of various view:
> Groves whose rich trees wept odorous gums and balm,
> Others whose fruit burnished with golden rind
> Hung amiable, Hesperian fables true,
> If true, here only and of delicious taste...   IV 246

The myth of the golden apples of the Hesperides drifts into Eden with no syntactical link, and we drift out of *PL* towards the classics on its vagueness – 'true, if true' – to be brought back sharply again with the local, physical 'taste'. In *PL*, taste is always a warning of the fall – but how did we reach it? Does it refer to the apples of Eden or of the Hesperides?

Narrative syntax

Sometimes Milton's syntax, though impressionistic, is peculiarly efficient:

> He ended, and they both descend the hill;
> Descended, Adam to the bower where Eve
> Lay sleeping ran before, but found her waked;
> And thus with words not sad she him received.   XII 606

He is *using* the tenses and participles to make a small syntactical model of a quite large and complicated series of events. Michael ending his speech, and his going down the hill with Adam, and their reaching the bottom, are merged by the rhymes in ended-descend-descended. Then we see Adam; the bower with Eve sleeping in it; Adam again, running towards it; the bower with Adam arrived and Eve awake. The last line is much slower, in the sense that it describes a much smaller event, thus emphasizing it; and the final clause, 'she him received', uses an alien word-order to as it were embrace *him* within *she* who is recEiVEd. We can almost draw a diagram of these syntactical operations:

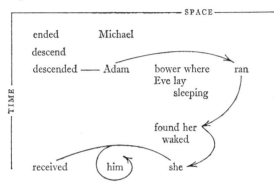

Syntax in speeches

It is when Milton uses syntax to carry ideas, rather than things and actions, that it is difficult to follow. This happens most often in speeches. If they have a strong argumentative line, they will seem the more awkward. This is a paradox; it happens because, although the self-embedding pattern of Milton's syntax is 'logical', or at any rate sequential, it is not a logic that comes naturally to us; because his own bent was towards impressionistic effects; and because the character's logic may in any case be fallacious. That is why the evil speeches, and God's, are the most difficult to follow.

It is best to read even them as a series of concepts flowing through the mind rather than as a logical sequence of ideas. When Beelzebub advises an attack on man rather than God, he uses a stream of consciousness kind of rhetoric as the apparently logical basis for his case:

> here perhaps
> Some advantageous act may be achieved
> By sudden onset, either with hellfire
> To waste his whole creation, or possess
> All as our own, and drive as we were driven,
> The puny habitants, or if not drive,
> Seduce them to our party, that their God
> May prove their foe, and with repenting hand
> Abolish his own works. This would surpass
> Common revenge, and interrupt his joy
> In our confusion, and our joy upraise
> In his disturbance...   II 362

In 1963 one of the English A-level examining boards, falling for Beelzebub's rhetoric, asked candidates to rewrite that part of his speech in modern prose. Let's try:

It is against this target [the new creation] that we might get somewhere by a blitzkrieg – we might either devastate the whole thing with hellfire, or take it over and expel the feeble inhabitants just as we were expelled – or if not expel them, get them onto our side so that their God will turn into their enemy. Then, sorry that he'd ever created them, he would abolish his own creation. That would be something more than ordinary revenge: it would stop him enjoying our defeat, and give us some pleasure.

But of course we lose just that sliding opportunism – 'and drive as we were driven...or if not drive, Seduce' – which is characteristic of hell's politics; and which is so weirdly represented under the paraphrasable crust of Milton's syntax.

The speeches most suited to Milton's style are the querulous complaints and cries of Adam and Eve. Eve, warned against being alone in the garden, replies in a way that can be represented as dramatic prose:

But that thou shouldst my firmness therefore doubt, to God or thee, because we have a foe may tempt it, I expected not to hear.	*Haughty, putting Adam in the wrong.*

His violence thou fear'st not, being such as we,
     not capable of death or pain, can either not
     receive, or can repel.
	*Confusing Adam
	 with a show
	 of logic.*

His fraud is then thy fear: which plain infers thy equal fear that my firm faith and love can by his fraud be shaken or seduced –	*More logic to prove that Adam has insulted her.*
thoughts which how found they harbour in thy breast,	*Smooth acceleration from logic to emotion; petulant turning away.*
Adam,	*Turning back.*
misthought of her to thee so dear?	*Stifled sobs.*

IX 279...

The syntax fits her hurried quarrelling voice. The last two lines are simply not English but it is the kind of thing we say when, convinced of our own right, we still suppress full rage; and still, in the sobs of the last six monosyllables, offer a possible reconciliation. There is much of this in IX and X. After the fall when Adam upbraids her Eve replies:

> What words have passed thy lips, Adam severe,
> Imput'st thou that to my default, or will
> Of wandering, as thou call'st it, which who knows
> But might as ill have happened thou being by,
> Or to thyself perhaps...   IX 1144

It has affinities with Molly Bloom's interior monologue at the end of Joyce's *Ulysses:* '...O much about it if thats all the harm ever we did in this vale of tears God knows its not much doesnt everybody only they hide it...'

Two-way syntax

Because Milton uses so many qualifiers – adjectives and adverbs – both before and after the noun or verb, and because he uses impressionistic syntax, his words sometimes work in two directions at once:

> Thus saying, from her husband's hand her hand
> Soft she withdrew...   IX 385

Is it that her hand was soft, or she withdrew it softly? Similarly, later in the same passage:

> O much deceived, much failing, hapless Eve,
> Of thy presumed return!   404

In fact she does not fail to return to Adam after the temptation; but when she returns she has failed to resist temptation, has indeed failed the whole human race. You cannot analyse these phrases into one meaning.

Miltonic syntax is often found in great prose-writers (see especially the descriptive prose of James and Conrad, and the stream of consciousness of Joyce's characters). But here is a case in Wallace Stevens's *Sunday morning*, a poem about paradise and 'that old catastrophe':

> Complacencies of the peignoir, and late
> Coffee and oranges in a sunny chair,
> And the green freedom of a cockatoo
> Upon a rug mingle to dissipate
> The holy hush of ancient sacrifice.

Do the circumstances of the Sunday morning woman mingle *in order to* dissipate the holy hush – a deliberate defence against its troubling? or do they have that effect willynilly? What meanings does *dissipate* have?

Rhetoric

Milton manipulated syntax as a form of metaphor. This is not peculiar to him: it is true of early 18th-century poetry. A highly syntactical, unmetaphorical style looks peculiar, however, in relation to Elizabethan poetry; yet the Elizabethans themselves recognized two distinct ways in which meaning might be changed and intensified: tropes and schemes. *Tropes* [= changes] include everything we now call imagery – metaphors, similes, metonymy, etc.: figures in which one thing stands for another. *Schemes* are arrangements of language rather than metamorphoses of meaning; anaphora, for example, is a scheme in which two or more lines begin with the same word. But schemes do sometimes have a tropal effect: when Pope says in the *Rape of the lock* that the sylphs look after Belinda lest she 'stain her honour or her new brocade', he is using a scheme called zeugma, in which one verb operates on two different objects; but the zeugma suggests that Belinda equates honour with brocade, a stain on her virginity with a stain on her dress, her virginity itself with mere outward show. Zeugma, the scheme, has invented a simile, which is a trope.

The Elizabethans used schemes a good deal but they tend to disappear under the more exciting tropes. In Milton's blank verse, they emerge. Because we are no longer familiar with schemes, it is necessary to use technical language to name them; but the names are of no importance. It is enough simply to be aware of the presence of rhetorical schemes in his verse.

Syntactical schemes

Most schemes are in some sense to do with syntax or grammar but the most complicated are purely syntactical. Here are a few:

Antimetabole. Repeating a phrase the other way round, e.g. v 623 about the dancing of the angels and the stars:

> mazes intricate,
> Eccentric, intervolved, yet regular
> Then most, when most irregular they seem.

Auxesis. Phrases arranged in a climactic order of sense, as with Raphael talking about the moon: 'Her spots thou seest As clouds, and clouds may rain, and rain produce Fruits in her softened soil, for some to eat Allotted there' (VIII 145).

Climax. Similar to auxesis: interlocking parallel constructions. The Father talking of the Son's offer to redeem man:

> So man, as is most just,
> Shall satisfy for man, be judged and die,
> And dying rise, and rising with him raise
> His brethren, ransomed with his own dear life. III 294

The speeches in heaven are very schematic, as if Milton were using the figures of rhetoric to represent the watertightness of divine logic. There is also a lot of schematic verse in the hymns that Adam and Eve sing to creation, and Raphael's descriptions to them of the universe; here rhetoric suggests the interrelatedness and formality of God's works:

> Thou sun, of this great world both eye and soul,
> Acknowledge him thy greater, sound his praise
> In thy eternal course, both when thou climb'st
> And when high noon hast gained, and when thou fall'st...
>
> V 171...

Iterative [=repeating] schemes

Rhyme. The amount of repetition and rhyme in that part of the hymn introduces schemes which repeat words. Milton uses these to preserve his verse from blankness. There is much more plain rhyme than at first appears: notice the rhymes on *light* in that hymn. 'Fall'st...fly'st... flies' is nearly a triple rhyme and it rhymes internally with other words. It also includes an odd trick of Milton's which may be called anti-rhyme, where words of opposite sense end successive lines. Here are some other iterative schemes:

Anadiplosis. Repetition of last words of first line at beginning of next:

> As I bent down to look, just opposite,
> A shape within the watery gleam appeared
> Bending to look on me, I started back,
> It started back, but pleased I soon returned,
> Pleased it returned as soon with answering looks
> Of sympathy and love... IV 460

The repetition 'mirrors' the reflection it describes.

Antistrophe. The renaissance rhetoricians used this word for various sorts of rhyme, but especially the repetition of a whole line, e.g. 'What better can we do, than to the place Repairing where he judged us, prostrate fall Before him reverent, and there confess...' at x 1086 – the whole sentence is repeated in the next paragraph when they actually do it.

Epanalepsis. Starting and ending a line, or pair of lines, with the same word: 'Sweet is the breath of morn, her rising sweet' (IV 641); 'but rather seek Our own good from our selves, and from our own Live to our selves' (II 252).

Ploce. Repetition of a single word for special effect. There is a very great deal of this; the most impressive example is Eve's cry of penitence at x 934, already quoted.

Prosonomasia. Like-sounding words close together, e.g. 'the King of glory in his powerful *Word* And Spirit coming to create new *worlds*' (VII 208). Cf. ordinary puns, especially frequent in V–VI, e.g. 'briefly touch What we propound' = fire cannon (VI 566 – the whole speech is a pun).

Traductio. Repetition of a word in an altered form, e.g. 'highly they raged Against the Highest' (I 667).

Minor components of epic

Epic was the senior genre. Certain habits of style came to be expected of it, rather as certain habits of behaviour take on an air of importance when a prince or a grandfather practises them, even though lots of ordinary people do too. In other words, epic throws its own details into relief; but once you have noticed them in epic you will find examples in many other poems as well.

Recurring epithets

Some of the minor conventions of epic were designed to help the bard chant from memory, sometimes perhaps ad-libbing, to a large audience. The most obvious case is the 'kenning' or fixed recurring epithet as in 'the wily Odysseus', 'rosy dawn'. In *PL* there is *dark* regularly applied to chaos (II 405 464 891 916 953 960 1027, III 11 424, VI 482 870, VII 212, X 283 371 438), *glorious* to angels, *gentle* breezes (IV 156 806, VIII 515, X 93), *winged* heralds and angels (I 752, III 299 IV 576, V 247 277 468, VII 199 572). Milton's use of this device is subtler than Homer's (and than his own 18th-century imitators'). His epithets shift round their nouns, altering rhythm and emphasis: 'the dark abyss', 'the dark unbottomed infinite abyss'. The noun itself changes: 'a dark illimitable ocean', 'rising world of waters dark and deep'. The adjective may be applied to abstract nouns: 'dark designs' (I 213), 'dark idolatries' (I 456), 'doubtful consultations dark' (II 486). Sometimes the epithet becomes a noun itself: 'all the coasts of dark' (II 464), 'the hollow dark' (II 953).

In a poem designed for literate reception, the recurring epithet has other effects as well. It produces noun units which are longer than usual; this slows up the action, for a constantly rosy dawn or fiery deluge leaves less room in line and sentence for other bits of syntax, especially for verbs – that is, for action. It has been found, in fact, that Milton's sentences are longer and have a higher proportion of adjectives, and of prepositions and conjunctions, than Shakespeare's and T. S. Eliot's. His sentences have fewer verbs than theirs and are more often passive. He was concerned, we might say, with qualification, description, category; and with what is done *to* A or B rather than with what X or Y do (see R. D. Emma *Milton's grammar* 1964).

Compound epithets

A feature of Greek, and suited Milton's emphatic defining style. E.g. 'row Of fruit-trees over-woody' (V 213), 'All perfect good unmeasured out' (V 399), 'virtue-proof' (V 384).

Chronographia

Heroic telling the time; elaborate punctuation marks for the long poem. Several in IV–VI e.g.

> Now morn her rosy steps in the eastern clime
> Advancing, sowed the earth with orient pearl,
> When Adam waked.   V I

Personification and metaphor

Chronographia nearly always personifies Morn, Dawn etc. because it makes an action out of the passing of time. This irritates us because we do not think of time – or death, sunshine, grace, truth, slander, peace – as powers acting in the world: we think of them more as names for events that are best described in terms of particles and waves, or as names for human actions.

If we must have personification, we prefer it to startle: 'My heart in hiding rebuffed the big wind' (Hopkins *Windhover*). The same with metaphor. But it is only recently that poets have aimed at originality of metaphor; and in epic, intensity of personification would clog the big public theme. It sometimes clogs in Shakespeare:

> Perséverance, dear my lord,
> Keeps honour bright; to have done, is to hang
> Quite out of fashion, like a rusty mail
> In monumental mockery. Take the instant way;
> For honour travels in a strait so narrow
> Where one but goes abreast: keep, then, the path;
> For Emulation hath a thousand sons
> That one by one pursue... *Troilus* III iii 150

That is too mixed a lot of metaphors and personifications to follow without much gesturing; but at least it is active. In epic you tend to meet static metaphors. Then, the more static, and the less animated, the better: 'deep on his front engraven Deliberation sat and public care' (II 302); 'and on his crest Sat horror plumed' (IV 988); 'Silence was pleased' (IV 604).

Usually, though, Milton's personifications are more animated than that – but less than the optimum: so we find ourselves puzzling over what seems to be an unattached metaphor, like 'holds' here:

> mean while murmuring waters fall
> Down the slope hills, dispersed, or in a lake,
> That to the fringèd bank with myrtle crowned
> Her crystal mirror holds, unite their streams. IV 260

You can excuse the confusion by saying Milton wants us to pause on 'holds'. You can say that wanton animation and multiplicity are right for paradise. You can say the confusing detail of myrtle and mirror belong to Venus and she always presides over blissful gardens. Yet I still feel that Milton often imbues his personifications with the wrong degree of vitality; and puts into their hands a clumsy set of attributes. Ultimately, the way you personify must be an index of how much at home, or how alien, you feel with life.

133

Personification and metaphor are intervolved, especially in *PL* because Milton avoided *it*. The words *it* and *its* were coming into use as neuter pronouns in the middle of the 17th century; but Milton stuck to the earlier use, of *his*, *her* etc. even for inanimates and abstracts. You hardly notice this in Shakespeare because he is so fluent, and so easy with the personifications and metaphors that result from it (though this is one of the main hidden difficulties in understanding him). You notice it in Milton because he did not write (except in *Comus* and his prose) at the Elizabethan level of animation; and metaphor was not his métier.

In paradise there are flowers and fruit 'with gay enamelled colours mixed' (IV 149). Milton is suggesting that the garden of Eden is God's art, and that we should think of it in terms of, say, Botticelli's painting of *Spring*. But the metaphor in *enamelled* was already hackneyed. Milton only makes it worse with *mixed* for it leads us to think about the palette when it would be more enhancing if he led us to think about colour. Later on:

> now gentle gales
> Fanning their odoriferous wings dispense
> Native perfúmes, and whisper whence they stole
> Those balmy spoils.

The words 'fanning...dispense...whisper...stole' produce an effect by sibilance, and by association with birds, quietness, stealth; but the actual metaphor and personification does not do much work; you may not even be able to say what they are. Here is another set of personifications from Adam's story of Eve's creation:

> To the nuptial bower
> I led her blushing like the morn: all heaven,
> And happy constellations on that hour
> Shed their selectest influence; the earth
> Gave sign of gratulation, and each hill;
> Joyous the birds; fresh gales and gentle airs
> Whispered it to the woods, and from their wings
> Flung rose, flung odours from the spicy shrub,
> Disporting, till the amorous bird of night
> Sung spousal, and bid haste the evening star
> On his hill top, to light the bridal lamp.   VIII 510

'Blushing like the morn' implies a face for the morn. We would probably want to avoid that and say 'dawn-fire-faced' or 'sunrise-skin' or just 'dawning'. You can invent alternatives for the more obvious personifications here; but would an epic contain them? Does it contain these, from after the flood?

134

the clouds were fled,
Driven by a keen north wind, that blowing dry
Wrinkled the face of deluge, as decayed.   XI 837

When God creates vegetation,

> He scarce had said, when the bare earth, till then
> Desért and bare, unsightly, unadorned,
> Brought forth the tender grass, whose verdure clad
> Her universal face with pleasant green,
> Then herbs of every leaf, that sudden flowered
> Opening their various colours, and made gay
> Her bosom smelling sweet; and these scarce blown,
> Forth flourished thick the clustering vine, forth crept
> The swelling gourd, up stood the corny reed
> Embattled in her field; add the humble shrub,
> And bush with frizzled hair implicit; last
> Rose as in dance the stately trees, and spread
> Their branches hung with copious fruit; or gemmed
> Their blossoms.   VII 313

Like Ovid, renaissance poets often imaged the earth as a woman's body; and, having less luxury than us, they delighted in decoration; but can we accept the face in the fourth line? The vine, gourd and especially the reed with its stiff-strained stem, are good because they are plain. The shrub continues the body image, still clumsy with its joke on pubic hair. One hardly has time to realize the dance of the trees – it is wasted (Milton often throws away an image which, if he had elaborated it, would have been excellent; he preferred to cram everything in, instead of concentrating on the significant detail). But the last clause, because it is separate, and slower, and not physiological, is fine: we see blossom coming out on the trees like jewels.

This passage is typical of the weaker Milton: using a convention clumsily, sliding in a deadpan joke, missing the chance to set the trees dancing, yet doing something with 'the corny reed' and 'gemmed Their blossoms'. Compare Pope's *Windsor Forest*, James Thomson's *Seasons*, and Wordsworth's early *Evening walk* or *Descriptive sketches*.

Inventiveness with metaphor, and freedom to use that inventiveness, are probably symptoms of general mental energy. Milton's metaphorical powers are usually kept latent or, if released, used under strict intellectual control. On the fifth day of creation he uses a highly functional set of metaphors about fish:

> part single or with mate
> Graze the sea weed their pasture, and through groves
> Of coral stray, or sporting with quick glance
> Show to the sun their waved coats dropped with gold,

135

> Or in their pearly shells at ease, attend
> Moist nutriment, or under rocks their food
> In jointed armour watch.   VII 403

He has taken a classical image, of fish as submarine sheep, and made it
feel right by insisting on it, by making us see the underwater world
as a feeding-place. Then he changes to an heraldic image, with fish
in tabards and, down below, lobsters as knights. Notice how the
valved shellfish 'attend Moist nutriment', the language Latinate and
inactive, while the crustaceans 'watch their food'.

Periphrasis

There are various kinds of periphrasis. All refer to an object indirectly
or by describing its qualities or a part of it or by giving it a special
title. In oral epic it slowed up the chant, making it easier to follow,
presumably (though this could be tested on tape).

To us, periphrasis seems facetious; and its contexts far from heroic.
People use it when they are embarrassed, whether in public – the
best man proposing a toast – or private. You may call a younger
brother's guinea-pigs his furry friends; or answer the phone with
'This is the Lord Warden of the Cinque Ports speaking'. I suppose
these habits are symptoms of a check or twist in feelings about the
brother or his pets or your own identity; we want to hide the reality
behind alliteration, abstraction, grandiose title, joke and exaggeration.
On all this see Freud in *The psychopathology of everyday life*.

It is a convention of epic to use periphrasis for natural objects:
'showery arch' (VI 759 rainbow), 'gems of heaven', the moon's
'train', 'moving fires' (IV 648, VII 87 stars), 'empyreal mansion'
(III 699 heaven), 'watery throng' (VII 297 fish). Some of these are
difficult to justify. If you feel that 'empyreal mansion' is ludicrously
inflated it may be because it so easily changes into its ludicrously flat
equivalent, 'sky-house'. But some of these phrases present the object
in a significant light. 'Showery arch' is not the equivalent of rain(y)
bow: it is more architectural, the bow as part of the world's structure,
God's promise built into the sky. The unfamiliar phrase may make
you think harder about the object than an ordinary naming would. To
fish, the sea is not just a mass of water; it is 'their watery residence'
(VIII 346). To call stars gems is to suggest God's artistry. The sun
is 'the prime orb' (IV 592). Many periphrases occur in the books
describing the world and its creation.

Probably the most difficult periphrasis to accept is the kind represented in 'jaculation dire' (vi 665), 'ill mansion' (vi 738), 'wondrous pontifice' (x 348), 'Through optic glass the Tuscan artist views' (i 288). Why not say hell, or even evil dwelling, instead of 'ill mansion'? If 'jaculation dire' is meant to impress, doesn't it rather oppress us with fatiguing lexicography? In some of these cases we shall mistake for poetic diction what was at the time the ordinary phrase: optic glass, for example, was modern, rather technical but plain English for telescope (and artist = technologist). In some cases a special reference may be operating: *mansion* was more familiar than it is now, with the simple meaning of place to live, dwelling; the phrase 'ill mansion' has an Italianate effect that Milton often produced to keep his epic from being insular; and it echoes the text 'In my Father's house are many mansions' (*John* xiv).

We can say, then, about this apparently irritating kind of periphrasis, that we must look at each case in context; watch for changes of register in words (from plain to obscure, art to science, homely to pompous etc.); watch for special effects. But we should also be prepared, if we're going to read the poem at all, to accept oddities. Milton puzzles and surprises. Great writers do:

Morose delectation Aquinas tunbelly calls this, *frate porcospino*. Unfallen Adam rode and not rutted. Call away let him: *thy quarrons dainty is*. Language no whit worse than his. Monkwords, marybeads jabber on their girdles: roguewords, tough nuggets patter in their pockets.   Joyce *Ulysses* ch. i

Often the cause of stunning complexity is anger – Joyce's anger here with Roman Catholicism, Milton's too in *pontifice*, the word identifying Sin and Death's bridge with the Pope. Often it is just violence: jaculation dire may be regarded as a scholarly yell, the epic BANG or POW.

Periphrasis and recurrence

Combine periphrasis with recurrence and you have this:

> So spake the eternal Father, and fulfilled
> All justice: nor delayed the wingèd saint
> After his charge received; but from among
> Thousand celestial ardours, where he stood
> Veiled with his gorgeous wings, up springing light
> Flew through the midst of heaven; the angelic choirs
> On each hand parting, to his speed gave way
> Through all the empýreal road; till at the gate
> Of heaven arrived, the gate self-opened wide
> On golden hinges turning, as by work
> Divine the sovereign Architect had framed.   v 246

God, heaven, angel(s) are repeated several times each, in varying phrases. This is even done for Raphael's promptness – 'nor delayed ...up springing light...his speed'. This is certainly epical: simple units (God, angels, speed) hammered into place and given a superficial complexity with the varying phrasing; the emphatic yet decorated description of obviousness. It is similar to Celtic manuscript illumination and indeed may be related to that art historically, for epic too was a product of bronze ages. It is also a characteristic of all heroic baroque art – Tiepolo, Bernini. But it seems also to have been characteristic of Milton personally. He delighted in repetition, circumlocution, decoration, emphasis. He expressed his energies, and projected his conflicts, in these ways. Of course there is something damaged, neurotic about the expression. At its worst it is the literary equivalent of one who hectors, shouts, says everything twice, insistently describes the obvious. We could guess at causes for such a person's behaviour; but we should also consider that perhaps he has made the best of a bad job – no worse anyway than we make of ourselves. He might even have turned his symptoms to advantage, as a fairground salesman or a sergeant does. Clearly cosmic epic was an advantageous arena for Milton to shout in; and the wonder of it is, if we are going to be personal, with what delicacy and variety he exercises a style which could so easily slip into thunder. He *uses* his style:

> *Straight* knew him all the bands
> Of angels under watch; and to his *state*
> And to his *message high* in honour rise;
> For on some *message high* they *guessed* him bound.
> Their glittering tents he *passed*, and now is come
> Into the *blissful* field, through groves of myrrh,
> And flowering odours, cassia, nard, and balm;
> A *wilderness* of *sweets*; for nature here
> *W*antoned as in her *p*rime, and *p*layed at *will*
> Her virgin fancies, *pour*ing forth more *sweet*,
> *Wild* above rule or art; en*or*mous *bliss*.   v 287

Renaissance poets and critics were more conscious of decoration than we are, and valued it as such. The emphatic recurrences of this passage were all recognized and named as official devices of rhetoric.

He said

One of the conventions of epic is a periphrastic way of saying 'he said':

> Whereto with speedy words the arch-Fiend replied.   I 256
> And with persuasive accent thus began.   II 118

>   To whom the patriarch of mankind replied.   v 506
>   And thus the filial Godhead answering spake.   VI 722

The full-stop after the formula, and the lack of quotation marks, are entirely conventional. But they do indicate that in epic characters do not make conversation: they make speeches. Their speeches are not so much an expression of themselves as a part of the poem, like the prayers in a liturgy. These lines, however, give some indication of tone. Sometimes they do more: the last line above displays both the unity of the Father and Son, and the distinction between them, by the formula SON answering = FATHER speaking. In Book IX, when Adam and Eve argue about gardening, the sentences between their speeches measure the widening gap between the speakers. 'And Eve first to her husband thus began' (204) – neutral, domestic; but

>   To whom the virgin majesty of Eve,
>   As one who loves, and some unkindness meets,
>   With sweet austere composure thus replied.   270

This goes on until line 377.

Titles and names

Milton's style, and epic convention, united in calling names. Varying titles were recognized as a device. Satan is 'the apostate angel', 'the arch-fiend', 'their dread commander', 'the wily adder'. In his turn he calls God 'Tyrant', 'Thunderer' and so on. Adam and Eve call God 'our nourisher', 'the high Creator'. They address each other as 'Fair consort', 'Daughter of God and man', 'Best image of myself and dearer half'; but after the fall it is plain Adam and Eve.

Here periphrasis is being used to affirm roles. At present this is out of fashion with us but it was not long ago that people called each other wife, master; we still say 'Waiter!'. If you work out some possible titles for a contemporary epic you will uncover roles and interactions which are hidden by our normal manners. In *PL* we may object, though, when these titles are assigned by Milton instead of the characters: if Satan is labelled 'arch-enemy' he is lessened as any too obviously labelled villain is.

When Satan addresses his troops he calls them multiple names – 'Thrones, dominations, princedoms, virtues, powers' (actually ranks in the angelic hierarchy); so does God (e.g. V 600). Allied to this is the simple roll-call of grand names, such as the idols at I 392; the heroes of classical epic and medieval romance at I 576 (that list is contained

in a simile; it is often done like that); the snakes at x 521. A final class
is the list that maps a panorama – of winds at x 695, of entire conti-
nents at xi 385. There Michael shows Adam a vision of

> all earth's kingdoms and their glory.
> His eye might there command wherever stood
> City of old or modern fame, the seat
> Of mightiest empire, from the destined walls
> Of Cambalu, seat of Cathaian khan
> And Samarkand by Oxus, Temir's throne,
> To Paquin of Sinaean kings, and thence
> To Agra and Lahore of great Mogul
> Down to the golden Chersonese...

This was a convention of epic too but we can ask, What does it mean
to so insistently name so much (remembering the magic of names)?
What would its modern equivalent be? Certainly we should think of
it in the light not only of epic but of heroic art in the 17th century –
Bernini's repeating pillars holding up the huge semicircular colonnade
of St Peter's, Rome, the parapet topped with giant figures; the
disturbing flaunts of puce, green, purple drapes, and revelations of
grotesque or distant irrelevancies in say Tiepolo (his painting of
Danae is a good example).

Litotes

Double negative: 'Dismiss them not disconsolate' (xi 113); 'And
never but in unapproachèd bliss Dwelt from eternity' (iii 4). To our
ears pompous; but Milton used litotes as another way of piling up
words, and controlling the sense. Many languages have more
repetitively negative constructions than English; there is a difference
between A and not-not-A. Milton uses it strongly in xi–xii as a model
of the balance between hope and despair that men must now live in –
'And thus with words not sad she him received' (xii 609).

Simile

Milton's small similes are often weak. Of Death he says,

> black it stood as night,
> Fierce as ten Furies, terrible as hell,
> And shook a dreadful dart.

Bentley, editing *PL* in 1732, objected that 'to make one person, Death, to be as fierce as ten Furies together smells of trivial and common chat; and then "terrible as hell" is quite ridiculous. The man did not attend, that the scene here is hell: so Death, was no more terrible than the place he sat in'. There seems to be not much point in the various brief similes for noise:

> Their rising all at once was as the sound
> Of thunder heard remote.   II 476

> He ended, and the heavenly audience loud
> Sung hallelujah, as the sound of seas,
> Through multitude that sung.   X 641

Yet the first evokes a noise that's sinister on earth; the second merges by mysterious syntax the sea with the multitudinous singing, rather as Wallace Stevens does in *The idea of order at Key West:*

> She sang beyond the genius of the sea.
> The water never formed the mind or voice,
> Like a body wholly body, fluttering
> Its empty sleeves; and yet its mimic action
> Made constant cry, caused constantly a cry,
> That was not ours although we understood,
> Inhuman, of the veritable ocean.

Perhaps, then, we should read Milton's similes as very short associative or symbolic poems.

Epic simile

But Milton is master of the most important minor convention of epic, the epic simile. An epic simile is one in which the image or 'ikon' is not just referred to, but elaborated, perhaps forming a complete scene or incident itself. (I shall refer to the *subject* in the poem; the *ikon* that is its image; and the *quality* they seem to have in common.)

Epic similes introduce materials not in the story, like the landscape backgrounds of renaissance portraits; Ghiberti's Bible scenes on the panels of the Baptistry doors in Florence; profane carved capitals in Gothic churches and profane margins in manuscripts. The scenes graven on Bronze Age shields are a special case of this. Homer described Achilles' shield in *Iliad* XVIII in such detail that it became a view of the cosmos through a window (the shield) which is itself seen through a nearer window (the poem). When we read Chapman's version we are seeing it through a third window still:

And first he [Vulcan] forged a huge and solid shield
Which every way did variant artship yield,
Through which he three ambitious circles cast,
Round the refulgent; and, without, he placed
A silver handle. Fivefold proof it was,
And in it many things with special grace
And passing artificial pomp were graven.
In it was earth's green globe, the sea and heaven,
The unwearied sun, the moon exactly round
And all the stars with which the sky is crowned,
The Pleiades, the Hyads and the force
Of great Orion, and the Bear, whose course
Turns her about his sphere observing him
Surnamed the Chariot, and doth never swim
Upon the unmeasured ocean's marble face
Of all the flames that heaven's blue veil enchase.
In it two beauteous cities he did build
Of divers-languaged men. The one was filled
With sacred nuptials and with solemn feasts
And through the streets the fair officious guests
Lead from their bridal chambers their fair brides
With golden torches burning by their sides.
Hymen's sweet triumphs were abundant there
Of youths and damsels dancing in a sphere,
Amongst whom masking flutes and harps were heard.
And all the matrons in their doors appeared
Admiring their enamoured braveries...

It is usually said that epic simile gives 'relief', or offers a glimpse of 'reality'; but why, in the middle of a poem about the exploits of your founding fathers and the philosophy of your world? It seems more likely that the appeal of the epic simile lies in its window-opening or perspective effect. In the first place there is pleasure in the mere opening of the window, as with cut-out Advent calendars. Secondly there would, at any rate for classical and renaissance audiences, be pleasure in the mere description of physical objects, on two counts: because the objects themselves were rare; and because mimesis – turning things into words – was a magical power. Thirdly, the epic simile twists the heroic world and the ordinary world against each other so that each may be seen in terms of the other: Virgil compares the ghosts of the dead on the shores of Lethe to a swarm of bees, and Dante to scared frogs; Homer compares a battle to a snowstorm. It is possible that contemporaries, who had been close to bees and frogs and exposed to snow, could thereby more readily accept what they had never seen, the ghosts and battle – but I doubt it: the imagination doesn't need an epic simile to help it see a ghost. I am not even sure that epic similes achieve in any important way what Kenneth Burke calls, in metaphor, 'perspective of incongruity' (*Permanence and change* Los Altos 1954). Do we more sharply query and register the nature of ghost or frog by seeing either in terms of the other?

On the whole, I think the effect of epic similes is dynamic: it is the actual change of focus that matters. It is not just a shift from ghosts to frogs but from dark to light, past to recent; and from the storyflow to the static picture-window; from dimmer flux to vivid still. Then back again. The still frame emphasizes the cinema quality of the flow; it reminds us, in fact, that the story is moving.

Of course these effects are not peculiar to simile. As Achilles' shield proves, they are available in other sorts of frame such as description; even in speeches so far as they open a window into a character's head. Anything, in fact, that interrupts – 'And then' (*puis, þa, iamque, interea* – Virgil's conjunctions show him struggling delicately with the problem of sequence), anything that punctuates the flow, helps to validate the sequence. There is no genuine cause why what happens next should happen next, especially in stories with such loosely woven incidents as epics have. Each simile makes a fresh start, and a fresh end. Always at the start and often at the end similes offer a fresh set of conjunctions: 'As when' instead of 'And then'. Sometimes the links are comparative – 'as huge as...so stretched out huge in length' (I 196) – but usually they play with space and time: 'Not that...nor that...nor where...but wide remote from' (IV 268); 'never since of serpent kind Lovelier, not those that...' (IX 504).

But of course the device is put to different uses. Keats has two large epic similes in *Hyperion*, 'Those green-robed senators of mighty woods' (I 72) and the 'dismal cirque Of Druid stones, upon a forlorn moor' (II 34). They hardly change the focus: the outdated gods have already been presented in stony terms, and the whole poem moves with the slow describing pace of the similes.

Arnold was careful to epicize *Sohrab and Rustum* with similes. They do change the focus, sometimes too sharply (e.g. the woman watching her maid lay the fire at line 302); but he often uses them to supply local colour to his Persian tale.

Psychologically, the epic simile is a kind of dream; and dreaming may be for fitting new information into the brain's programmes. Arthur Hugh Clough treated simile as dream. He was the friend for whom Arnold wrote *Thyrsis*. His poem *The bothie of Tober-na-Vuolich: a vacation pastoral* (1848) is about some undergraduates on a reading-party in the Highlands of Scotland. One of them, Philip, falls in love with a local girl, Elspie. He makes a pass at her one evening but next day she rejects him (Canto vii):

> She paused, but quickly continued,
> Smiling almost fiercely, continued, looking upward.
> You are too strong, you see, Mr Philip! just like the sea there,
> Which *will* come, through the straits and all between the mountains,
> Forcing its great strong tide into every nook and inlet,
> Getting far in, up the quiet stream of sweet inland water,
> Sucking it up, and stopping it, turning it, driving it backward,
> Quite preventing its own quiet running...
>
> .   .   .   .
>
> That was what I dreamt all last night. I was the burnie,
> Trying to get along through the tyrannous brine, and could not;
> I was confined and squeezed in the coils of the great salt tide, that
> Would mix-in itself with me, and change me...

The simile provides local colour but its chief function is to open a window in Elspie's head, in fact to relate her dream. It seems likely that Clough tells the dream inside a simile so as to disguise, and to control, its symbolism. When Philip writes to his tutor later in the poem, he uses the same ikon:

> As at return of tide the total weight of ocean,
> Drawn by moon and sun from Labrador and Greenland,
> Sets-in amain, in the open space betwixt Mull and Scarba,
> Heaving, swelling, spreading, the might of the mighty Atlantic;
> There into cranny and slit of the rocky, cavernous bottom
> Settles down, and with dimples huge the smooth sea-surface
> Eddies, coils, and whirls; by dangerous Corryvreckan:
> So in my soul of souls through its cells and secret recesses,
> Comes back, swelling and spreading, the old democratic fervour.   IX

Clough develops them into a modern simile, of dawn flooding a city; but the import remains sexual. The sea and the rocky slits are symbols masquerading as epic simile; while with the description of the city at dawn Clough practically abandons the form of simile – it is impossible to hold any comparison in one's mind.

Although modern poets don't use epic simile much, their symbolism may amount to the same thing. One of Baudelaire's poems on *Spleen* starts:

> Je suis comme le roi d'un pays pluvieux,
> Riche, mais impuissant, jeune et pourtant très-vieux,
> Qui, de ses précepteurs méprisant les courbettes,
> S'ennuie avec ses chiens comme avec d'autres bêtes...

I am like the king of a rainy country, rich but powerless, young yet impotent: despising the care of tutors and as bored with his hounds as with all other creatures...

But in another spleen poem, 'J'ai plus de souvenirs que si j'avais mille ans', he omits the comparing *comme* and says simply, 'Je suis un cimetière...', 'Je suis un vieux boudoir...'. That became the usual 20th-century method; but in *Four quartets* Eliot reverted to a series of epic similes:

> I said to my soul, be still, and let the dark come upon you
> Which shall be the darkness of God. As, in a theatre,
> The lights are extinguished, for the scene to be changed
> With a hollow rumble of wings, with a movement of darkness on
>   darkness,
> And we know that the hills and the trees, the distant panorama
> And the bold imposing façade are all being rolled away –
> Or as, when an underground train, in the tube, stops too long
>   between stations
> And the conversation rises and slowly fades into silence...
>
> *East Coker* iii

Epic similes tend to raise theorizing. To get to more practical grips, consider the use of backgrounds in surrealist painting; and the way surrealist and pop painters juxtapose objects so as to suggest analogies between them. Then consider how the narrative is pushed along in narrative film, or radio drama for example. What apertures are made in the storyflow of modern forms?

Milton's similes are more frequent, longer, more complex and more meaningful than those of any other epic poet. For example, when Satan has escaped from hell up through chaos, he arrives on the outside shell of the universe; 'the firm opacous globe of this round world...a globe far off It seemed, now seems a boundless continent' smitten by dark tempests. He tries to find a way in:

> Here walked the Fiend at large in spacious field.
> As when a vulture on Imáus bred,
> Whose snowy ridge the roving Tartar bounds,
> Dislodging from a region scarce of prey
> To gorge the flesh of lambs or yeanling kids
> On hills where flocks are fed, flies towards the springs
> Of Ganges or Hydaspes, Indian streams;
> But in his way lights on the barren plains
> Of Sericána, where Chineses drive
> With sails and wind their cany waggons light:
> So on this windy sea of land, the Fiend
> Walked up and down alone bent on his prey.   III 430

For the 17th-century reader the mere materials were valuable. Milton is retailing information he had gathered from wide reading in recent travel books (as he is, for instance, in the similes of the Indian

Ocean and Abyssinia at IV 159 and 280); we would put it into text-books, films, television but they lacked those media. So they learned in the epic that vultures fly south from central Asia to feed off herds pasturing on the southern slopes of the Himalayas, where the Ganges and the Jelum (in the Punjab) rise; and that on a plateau in south-west China the inhabitants use a kind of sand-yacht. But the materials have significance in the story. Evil was thought to come from the north. Satan is repeatedly associated with oriental barbarians (X 431, II 3, I 717) and with birds of prey. The Ganges and Hydaspes were taken for the rivers Pison and Gihon which run out of Eden in *Genesis* ii 10–14 and *PL* IV 233. The 'hills where flocks are fed' suggest Satan's goal in *PL*, the pastoral garden of Eden, and the shepherd stories of the New Testament. When Satan does get there he leaps in with a related simile,

> As when a prowling wolf,
> Whom hunger drives to seek new haunt for prey,
> Watching where shepherds pen their flocks at eve.   IV 183

And, flying into the Tree of Life, he sits there 'like a cormorant' (196). The 'windy sea of land' takes part in the long series of maritime images for Satan's voyage; and the distortion of his environments (cf. 'palpable obscure'). But the air of the whole thing is more important than these details: the weird alien glimpses, presented with such documentary detail, adjust the focus of our reading eyes; and when the window shuts – 'So on this windy sea of land, the Fiend Walked up and down alone bent on his prey' – it pushes us on into the tale.

In proportion to their length, the books of *PL* with most epic similes are I, IV and IX. Book VIII has none, Books III, VII and X–XII very few. On the other hand, III and VII are rich in ordinary similes; VI and VII, active with war and creation, have an extraordinary number of metaphors.

One of the reasons Satan weighs so heavily in the poem is that he has more epic similes, and other imagery, attached to him than any other subject in the poem. Many of his ikons are distinctly of this world – classical giants and monsters, eclipses, comets, stars, ships, geography, animals and birds. The qualities most imaged are his size and his actions. The Father and Son have no epic similes – how could they? Eve has a number, but her ikons are mostly classical goddesses.

It is worth examining here, as a further example, a trio of epic similes concerned with peasants. They are at the ends of Books I, IV and XII. The first is a simile for the huge number of fallen angels who,

though 'they but now...seemed In bigness to surpass Earth's giant
sons Now less than smallest dwarfs', throng Pandemonium, like

> fairy elves,
> Whose midnight revels, by a forest side
> Or fountain some belated peasant sees,
> Or dreams he sees, while overhead the moon
> Sits arbitress, and nearer to the earth
> Wheels her pale course, they on their mirth and dance
> Intent, with jocund music charm his ear;
> At once with joy and fear his heart rebounds.   I 781

In the 17th century it was not ridiculous for an educated person to
half-believe in fairies; they were used a good deal in literature – *A
Midsummer Night's Dream*, Jonson's *Masque of Oberon* for the Prince
of Wales, Purcell's operas, both of Herrick's *Oberon* poems, laugh-
ingly by Pope in *The rape of the lock*. We know from *Comus* that
Milton liked this kind of fantasy. But what is it doing in *PL*? It
would seem to be mainly a transition from the volcanic eruptions of
Book I. But as it images the magical tininess of the fallen angels in
Pandemonium, it also diminishes their moral stature, from heavenly
beings to fairies, from devils to a superstition; and the muddled
peasant suggests that Satan's tremendous leadership is, in the end,
irrelevant to ordinary human nature. This simile is Milton's way of
labelling his hell as a poetic fiction.

The second peasant appears when Satan defies Gabriel and his
guard, who have arrested him in the garden of Eden:

> While thus he spake, the angelic squadrons bright
> Turned fiery red, sharpening in moonèd horns
> Their phalanx, and began to hem him round
> With ported spears, as thick as when a field
> Of Ceres ripe for harvest waving bends
> Her bearded grove of ears, which way the wind
> Sways them; the careful ploughman doubting stands
> Lest on the threshing-floor his hopeful sheaves
> Prove chaff. On the other side Satan alarmed
> Collecting all his might dilated stood,
> Like Teneriffe or Atlas unremoved;
> His stature reached the sky, and on his crest
> Sat horror plumed.   IV 977

This is an oddly various image, uncertain as the action. Although the
guardian angels have caught Satan, God hangs out his golden scales
in the sky and weighs the issue; shows that Satan would lose the
fight, but lets him escape. The squadron turns into a crescent moon;
there is a clause of very ordinary language – 'began to hem him

round'; then the squadron turns into a decorative field of barley waving in the wind. Ceres is not used as the corn-goddess but as a synonym for corn. There seem to be too many words – 'waving bends...Sways' – and they seem too ornate – 'bearded grove of ears'. It is typical of Milton to seem to be merely decorating but to be using his décor to insist on the actual: the words work together to make us realise in our minds the curious mixed qualities of a field of windblown corn – the stalks solid and stiff as a grove, yet flexible, with sharp hairy tops. Then without any logical connection such as 'When this happens' we see the ploughman watching his field and wondering if the wind will beat the ears of corn to chaff. What has this to do with Gabriel and Satan? It stands in a general way for the uncertainty of paradise: Adam and Eve may fall – they are free to; they may not – they do not have to. God preserves that perilous balance by releasing Satan now. Against this uncertainty Satan is gigantic. As usual, he is like a mountain; and the plumes on his helmet are a terrifying destructive version of the bristles on the barley. Yet the threshing simile also applies, in a devious way, to him, for he is going to be like Nebuchadnezzar's idol which was 'broken to pieces together, and became like the chaff of the summer threshing-floors; and the wind carried them away' (*Daniel* ii 35). Very shortly, when his power is weighed in the heavenly scales, Satan is going to be like Belshazzar at his feast, 'weighed in the balances, and found wanting' (*Daniel* v 27).

But beyond all these details stands the ploughman and his peaceful concerns, the representative of ordinary men. He reappears at the end of the poem when angels occupy the garden of Eden and Michael hurries Adam and Eve out:

> from the other hill
> To their fixed station, all in bright array
> The cherubim descended; on the ground
> Gliding meteorous, as evening mist
> Risen from a river o'er the marish glides,
> And gathers ground fast at the labourer's heel
> Homeward returning.   XII 626

This is not just a simile for the way the angels move. It implies that for Adam and Eve the spiritual world has become sinister; and as they leave paradise they are no longer lords of creation but like a tired peasant going home – a peasant whose 'grand parents' they are. So the poem runs into our world.

Milton's epic similes, then, are not pictures. On the other hand,

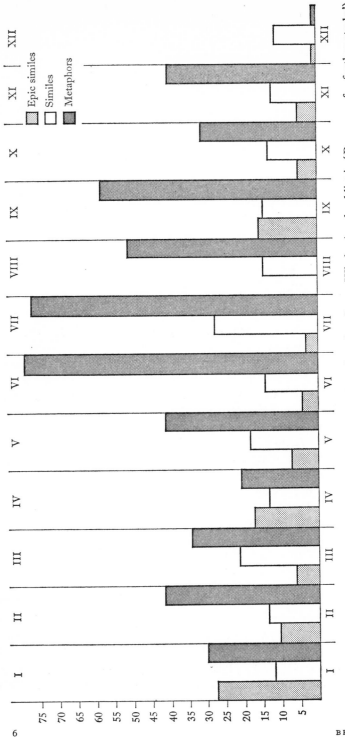

Distribution of epic similes, similes and metaphors in *Paradise Lost*, based on James Whaler (see booklist in 'Resources for further study')

they will not provide one-for-one images all through: you can say the angels are like mist, but not that paradise is like a marsh. Feel for the general atmosphere of an epic simile – violent, weird, mundane; and then ask what the various elements in it – fairies, Tartars, vultures, ploughmen – might be doing in relation to the subject of the simile, and in the epic at large.

Rhythm

When you read Milton's verse, relax: the syntax will unwind if you let it. Leave the unstressed syllables neutral; but notice that major stresses often provide internal rhyme:

> *Dar*kened so, yet shone
> Above them all the *arch* angel: but his face
> Deep sc*ars* of thunder had entrenched, and care
> Sat on his faded cheek, but under brows
> Of dauntless courage, and considerate pride
> Waiting revenge.   I 599

There are also consonant links in ar*ch*...entren*ch*ed...*ch*eek... cour*age*...reven*ge*.

These lines, which all happen to end with a monosyllabic word, indicate how important it is to determine rhythm by sense, not by respect for the theoretical ti-tum-ti-tum of iambic pentameters: *face | Deep scars* of *thun*der had en*trenched*, and *care | Sat*. At the end of each line you usually need a pause equivalent to a whole unsounded stress: for example, you must give CONSIDERATE PRIDE time to expand so that WAITING REVENGE becomes part of Satan as a whole, not just a characteristic of his pride.

Always obey the punctuation (which in this edition is Milton's own) even when it seems odd. If you try to rationalize Milton's punctuation you wreck his impressionistic syntax:

> from morn
> To noon he fell, from noon to dewy eve,
> A summer's day; and with the setting sun
> Dropped from the zenith like a falling star,
> On Lemnos the Aegáean isle.   I 742

Milton does not mean it to be the analysis of a sequence and the location of a place, 'from...to...and then', but the representation of free fall, re-entry and landing. He does not want us to think 'he dropped, like a falling star drops', but to receive in one piece something like SUNSETTING SKYFALL SHOOTING-STAR AIRDROPPING. Milton was aiming quite often at the way James Joyce wrote, or Hopkins when he used phrases like 'the sodden-with-its-sorrowing heart... The heaven-flung, heart-fleshed, maiden-furled Miracle-in-Mary-of-flame, Mid-numbered He in three of the thunder-throne!' (*Wreck of the Deutschland* xxvii...xxxiii). Similarly, he does not want us in the last line to register 'Lemnos, oh yes, that's an island in the Aegaean sea', but LEMNOS-THE-AEGAEAN-ISLE as words for a destination.

This habit of style, and the need to go with the rhythm, oppose the other need to think about individual words. As we have seen, Milton often uses words with special force – most often etymological force. When that force is ignored, his language seems dull; but attending to it may impede the rhythm. For example,

Next Chemos, the óbscene dread of Moab's sons   I 406

The unusual stressing of *obscene* and the internal rhyme with Chemos, as well as the periphrasis for the Moabites, distract us from *dread* and let us think it means 'what they were frightened of'; but it doesn't: it means an object of awe, especially an idol. Milton is using the word to remind us of the peculiar relation between the holy and the obscene, sacred and profane – both are taboo, in different senses dreadful.

Milton had a special gift for expressing violent muscular activity, and his epic often calls for it on a giant scale, so one of the most familiar Miltonic rhythms is an effortful spasm of stresses:

Fórthwíth úpríght he reárs from óff the póol	7 stresses
His míghty státure	I 221
on smóoth the séal,	
And bénded dólphins pláy: párt húge of búlk	6 stresses; note
	PART HUGE
Wállowing unwiéldy, enórmous in their gáit	4 stresses
Témpest the ócean	VII 409

That second piece is another example of Milton's curious way of handling clauses: you can read it as 'the seal and bended dolphins play on the smooth surface of the sea', but it is better to follow the punctuation and read it more like SMOOTH-SURFACE-SEAL, PLAY-BENDING-DOLPHINS. Similarly in the next bit, about whales, you might be expected to paraphrase it as 'Some, who are of huge size and wallow unwieldy and take enormous strides, raise storms in the ocean'. But that misses both Milton's impressionistic syntax (it's the bulk that wallows) and his particular kind of rationality, which does not bother with who...and...therefore. It should go something more like this: 'Some are so huge of bulk that they wallow unwieldy like a fat old boat; but when they move it's like a giant fording a river, they

151   6-2

raise tempests in what is itself tempestuous.' Again, one word, *tempest*, contains a lot.

Another of Milton's most characteristic rhythms is a version of the muscular effort in which he imitates the sound of an organ. He does this explicitly at XI 556, and covertly at the end of the creation of the world:

> The heavens and all the constellations rung,
> The planets in their stations listening stood,
> WHILE the BRIGHT POMP asceNDed JUBilANT.   VII 562

Another strong but quieter rhythm is 'Shoots invisible virtue even to the deep' (III 586 about sunshine), where there is a heavy pause between almost every word. This leads us to the heavy mourning tone that Milton sometimes uses: 'His sad exclusion from the doors of bliss' (III 525) and, about paradise being washed out to sea by the flood, 'The haunt of seals and orcs, and sea-mews' clang' (XI 831), or, about Satan being wounded, 'And all his armour stained erewhile so bright' (VI 334; this imitates the rhythms of Elizabethan verse; cf. XI 836 and much of VII).

Milton's more flexible, lyrical passages are often touched with this note of high nostalgic lament: obviously in such lines as

> bring back
> Through the world's wilderness long wandered man
> Safe to eternal paradise of rest   XII 312

but also in erotic and pastoral contexts:

> I nearer drew to gaze;
> When from the boughs a savoury odour blown,   *active*
> Grateful to appetite, more pleased my sense   *vegetable, nose*
> Than smell of sweetest fennel, or the teats   *cadence*
> Of ewe or goat dropping with milk at even,   *animal, mouth*
> Unsucked of lamb or kid, that tend their play.   IX 578

Milton's verse is famous for being extreme, for representing the violent, huge, exotic – 'the blasted stars looked wan' (X 412), 'Giants of mighty bone, and bold emprise' (XI 638), 'Sails between worlds and worlds' (V 268). But his most interesting verse, and his most subtle rhythms, occur when he is using that violence more personally, not in an exotic context but one where the language is simplified by the sturdy naturalness of 'bring back', 'dropping with milk', 'a summer's day'. These contexts are not usually active but moral or psychological, especially invocations, and laments for sin, weakness and tyranny:

> Tyranny must be,
> Though to the tyrant thereby no excuse.   XII 95

From man's effeminate slackness it begins,
Said the angel, who should better hold his place
By wisdom, and superior gifts received.
But now prepare thee for another scene.   XII 630

Style

By now we have passed beyond any particular element and are talking
about style in general, and therefore, in the end, about Milton or
ourselves:

While [Shakespeare] darts himself forth, and passes into all the forms of
human character and passion...[Milton] attracts all forms and things to
himself, into the unity of his own ideal.

COLERIDGE Biographia literaria ch. 15

It is no good expecting 'sensitivity' from Milton; but you can expect
definiteness. 'Manlike, but different sex' (VIII 471) is a definition of
women that ignores the ornate superfices – what he calls 'these
troublesome disguises which we wear' and by which we usually
judge sex; it outlines the form of mankind with *manlike* and then
differentiates it with *sex* (the word then meaning genitals, and gender,
rather than sexual emotion or action, of course). You meet the same
definiteness in 'the bought smile Of harlots' (IV 765), 'The cattle in
the fields and meadows green' (VII 460), and in Eve after her nightmare:

> and she was cheered,
> But silently a gentle tear let fall
> From either eye, and wiped them with her hair;
> Two other precious drops that ready stood
> Each in their crystal sluice, he ere they fell
> Kissed as the gracious signs of sweet remorse
> And pious awe, that feared to have offended.   V 129

'And she *was* cheered' it goes – domestic emphasis in epic. Consider
the role of imagery and decoration in these other versions of the topic:

> and as she spake
> Forth from those two tralucent cisterns brake
> A stream of liquid pearl, which down her face
> Made milk-white paths, whereon the gods might trace
> To Jove's high court...   MARLOWE *Hero and Leander*

153

Here overcome, as one full of despair
She veiled her eyelids, who, like sluices, stopped
The crystal tide that from her two cheeks fair
In the sweet channel of her bosom dropped;
    But through the floodgates breaks the silver rain,
    And with his strong course opens them again.

SHAKESPEARE Venus and Adonis

      Those happy smilets
That played on her ripe lip seemed not to know
What guests were in her eyes, which parted thence
As pearls from diamonds dropped.   *Lear*

With that adown out of her crystal eyne
Few trickling tears she softly forth let fall,
That like two orient pearls did purely shine
Upon her snowy cheek; and therewithal
She sighèd soft...
.   .   .   .
Wiping the tears from her suffusèd eyes...

SPENSER Fairy Queen

Whatever conclusions you may come to about those versions you are likely to agree that Milton's is closest to Spenser's; but stiffer, and its decor more solid and exact – crystal sluice is not so much a metaphor as a delineation of that shiny cusp at the eye's inner edge where tears well. The simplicity is domestic and plain – 'and wiped them with her hair'. The elements are conceived in separation rather than intrinsicately as in the *Lear* piece – 'Two other precious drops...' The syntax is as we have already seen passive, clausal, suspended – drops (that...) he (ere...) kissed (as...). 'Imagery' is less important than the emblematic value of the materials (Mary Magdalene) and the dry symbolism of the words (*fall...fell*, rhyming). All things and ideas are fixed, defined as their 'real' Platonic selves by unalterable epithets – gentle tear, precious drops, sweet remorse, pious awe.

If you translate all that into a syndrome you have to say it represents a soul self-punitively bent on binding the liquid and intimate in safe rigour. Richly aware of the hair, the eyes, the water in himself, and his experience of others and the world, he feared them as symbols of a power that would entangle, overwhelm and drown him if left unbound. The story is told again in *Lycidas* (again with hair and water), in *Comus* (the name means hairy), in *Samson*, and over several poems in his allusions to the myths of Orpheus and Thammuz, who were torn and eaten by an orgy of women and their remains thrown into a river:

> But drive far off the barbarous dissonance
> Of Bacchus and his revellers, the race
> Of that wild rout that tore the Thracian bard
> In Rhódopë, where woods and rocks had ears
> To rapture, till the savage clamour drowned
> Both harp and voice; nor could the Muse defend
> Her son.   VII 32

A great deal of Milton's way of organizing language, and hence experience, including the experience of himself, can be regarded as defence against the savage clamour. See also *Nativity Ode* 181, *Lycidas* 38, *Comus* 205 550, *PL* I 446.

In his most personal passages, the invocations, simple definiteness combines with the note of lament, and the tendency to hector, and his anxieties, to produce extraordinary poetry. It is centred on a personality without being egotistical or elegiac; it may include exotic materials but they are tempered, just as everyday materials are enriched, by the great pressure of his rhythms. Here Milton achieves what can only be called 'puritan' verse in the highest sense.

> Thus with the year
> Seasons return, but not to me returns
> Day, or the sweet approach of even or morn,
> Or sight of vernal bloom, or summer's rose,
> Or flocks, or herds, or human face divine;
> But cloud instead, and ever-during dark
> Surrounds me, from the cheerful ways of men
> Cut off...   III 40

Rhetoric, and the special stress that a line's first word receives, are used very delicately in the first three lines to contrast the external passage of the seasons with his internal immobility of night. With 'the sweet approach of even or morn' you think you are starting an unremarkable catalogue, till you notice how the flat words are being enriched: *sweet* sounds obvious; but how can an approach be sweet? The abstract noun gives life to the physical adjective; characteristically, Milton does not hint at but only allows you if you wish to provide the image that lurks below, of dawn and twilight like the sweetening approach of a woman. 'Vernal bloom' is conventional, yet its meaning emerges in relation to 'summer's rose': the pattern is one of Latin generality for spring flowers narrowing to a specific flower in the native summer. Again in the next line, the general many-words for sheep and cattle are suddenly broken open by the extraordinary phrase 'human face divine'; the amphibian position of man between animal and angel is represented by *human* in the native

155

position, before the noun, and *divine* in the alien position, after it; yet the phrase is so solid that human = divine where faces are concerned.

Conclusion

Let us end with a fairly neutral passage which has none of Milton's more exotic peculiarities, but much of the basic sinew of his way of writing. Zephon, one of the angels guarding paradise, finds Satan intruding. He does not recognize Satan and asks him who he is:

> Know ye not then said Satan, filled with scorn
> Know ye not me? IV 827

– a good illustration of Milton almost obliterating punctuation so as to incorporate tone of voice in the slow heroic narrative. Zephon replies that Satan is no longer fully angelic:

> Think not, revolted spirit, thy shape the same,
> Or undiminished brightness, to be known
> As when thou stood'st in heaven upright and pure.

'Or undiminished brightness' has no syntactical connection with 'Think not'; it is a typical Miltonic compression. Then Zephon arrests Satan:

> So spake the cherub, and his grave rebuke
> Severe in youthful beauty, added grace
> Invincible: abashed the Devil stood,
> And felt how awful goodness is, and saw
> Virtue in her shape how lovely, saw, and pined
> His loss; but chiefly to find here observed
> His lustre visibly impaired; yet seemed
> Undaunted. IV 844

We have the usual compression of syntax into a set of concepts – youthful beauty + grave rebuke severe = invincible grace. At the same time there is great simplicity: 'abashed the Devil stood, And felt...'. There is little decoration, but the lines are being manipulated strongly – *saw* spreads out at the end of the fourth line and rhymes in the fifth; the sixth and seventh lines start with a sort of anti-anaphora – 'His loss [which was of] His lustre'. Along with the simplest possible diction – 'stood...felt...and saw...and pined' – there is a high proportion of negatives and prefixes: *in*vincible, *im*paired, *un*daunted. Indeed, the proportion of abstract words is particularly high. Typically, a physical encounter is presented in abstract terms, as, when Satan and Michael engage in single combat, 'expectation stood In horror' (VI 306). At a more general level, it is also typical that the encounter is presented as a moral issue – invincible grace versus undaunted loss. The terms are antithetical, yet like-sounding; and the issue is insoluble except by some unimaginable transcendent power because it is between an irresistible force and an immovable object.

It is from this tendency of Milton's to give like-sounding names to opposing concepts, and then make them clash against each other irreconcilably, that we receive the impression of something unresolved, of a talent antagonistic to itself, which critics often remark on in respect of a detail – the heroism of Satan and the anti-heroic rejection of him, for example; the pervading classicism, and the rejection of classical culture; the hypnotic persuasions of Comus, and Sabrina's magic harmonies. This, ultimately, is what *PL* is about. Milton solves the conflict at the end of the poem only by a quiet unanimity between Adam and Eve which resigns itself to loss and submits itself to what appears to be the stronger of the two ultimate powers.

That is as far as it is profitable to go in answering the question, 'What is the meaning of *PL*?' Even in a small poem, 'meaning' can mean all sorts of things – what it means to me, what I think the poet meant, what the poem seems to stand for. In a large poem, the question is even vaguer, especially in *PL* where Satan diminishes in stature all the way through and drops out two books before the end; and where the last two books – which must by their position at the end be powerful in determining the poem's residual effect – are mostly about things which haven't happened yet. Certainly it is pointless even to ask, 'Did Milton succeed in justifying the ways of God to men?' All you can say is that the poem is about the conflict of ultimate forces over man; and then you may begin to make further small propositions or ask questions of detail: perhaps the conflict over man represents a conflict in man? What are the characteristics of the two ultimate forces? Apparently most people agree that Milton's way of writing is suited to the representation of conflict; is it also suited to other states? Most of us are likely to agree that if the poem 'proves' anything it is only in the sense that it exhibits God as possessing, in the end, a marginal superiority of power, and virtue, over Satan – as if Milton were bent on assuring himself that the forces of invincible grace and undaunted loss are not irreconcilable, but that grace will help loss if loss will surrender its undauntedness.

Resources for further study

Meant for students up to about the first postgraduate year. Material of interest mainly to professional scholars, or unlikely to be digested by students, excluded. On the whole, assume that if a work has been excluded it has been excluded deliberately; but the same is true of inclusions, even if unfamiliar; e.g. Sewell's *Study in Milton's Christian doctrine*, or M. M. Ross's works, which don't get paperbacked, are excellent. The only paperback of critical essays worth individual purchase is *Milton's epic poetry* ed Patrides 1967 Penguin – excellent.

This list concentrates on *PL*; for other aspects of Milton, and for most general, background and historical studies, see one of the bibliographies listed below or *John Milton: introductions* in this series.

Place of publication London and/or New York unless specified. Chapter and article titles in roman within quotation marks, book and periodical titles in italic. SMITH 'chapter title' *book title* 1968 means Smith wrote the whole book; if he didn't, it will be followed by an editor's name, or periodical volume and page numbers.

Annotated editions
PL general
PL topics
Sources and composition of *PL*
Illustrations to *PL*

* Art and iconography
Film and TV
Speech
* Music and dance

* Milton's influence
* Literary history
Epic and mythology
Religion
* History of ideas, science, Weltanschauung
Geography
History
Reference
Bibliography

* See also chapters in *John Milton: introductions* in this series.

Annotated editions of PL in chronological order

The most generously and gracefully annotated edition is that by M. Y. Hughes 1962: see details below. But a look at the notes to an *early* edition is one of the best ways of finding out what Milton felt like to the 17th and 18th centuries. It can also spark off study of your own.

HUME, PATRICK ed *Poetical works* 5 parts 1695.

BENTLEY, RICHARD ed *PL* 1732. See Wm. Empson, 'M and Bentley' *Some versions of pastoral* 1935 and R. M. Adams, 'Empson and Bentley' *Ikon: JM and the modern critics* Ithaca N.Y. 1955.

NEWTON, THOS. ed *Poetical works* 3 vols 1749–52 and various reprints. Illustrated by Hayman. Reprint with illustrations by Doré and others New York 1936.

TODD, H. J. ed variorum *Poetical works* 6 vols 1801; 7 vols 1809.

MASSON, DAVID ed *Poetical works* 3 vols 1874 rev 1890.

VERITY, A. W. ed *The Cambridge M for schools* 10 vols Cambridge 1891–6, rev ed of *PL* 1910, another 1921 with notes available separately.

PATTERSON, F. A. ed *The student's M* 1930 rev 1933. Complete poems and much prose in one big vol on thin paper.

HUGHES, MERRITT Y. Various editions of *PL* separately, and as part of works, published by Odyssey Press, New York, since 1935. The latest edition of *M: complete poems and major prose* is 1957, of which *PL* has most recently been revised and published separately in paper in 1962. This is the best annotated edition.

CAREY, JOHN and FOWLER, ALASTAIR ed *The poems of JM* 1968. Longmans Annotated English Poets gen ed F. W. Bateson. All in one fat vol. *PL* ed Fowler.

PATRIDES, C. A. is general ed of a multi-vol edition for schools being published by Macmillan.

PL general

ADAMS, ROBERT M. ch 6 'M's verse: efforts at a judgement', and ch 7 'Conclusion: M and magnanimity' *Ikon: JM and the modern critics* Ithaca N.Y. 1955.

BROADBENT, J. B. *Some graver subject: an essay on PL* 1960. Ch on heaven repr *M's epic poetry* ed Patrides 1967.

CAREY, JOHN *Milton* Literature in Perspective Series 1969.

COLERIDGE, S. T. Milton in Lecture X on Donne, Dante, M, *PL* in his course of lectures (1818). *Essays and lectures on Shakespeare etc.* Everyman.

EMPSON, WILLIAM *M's God* 1961. Ch on Eve repr *M's epic poetry* ed Patrides 1967.

HANFORD and TAAFE *Milton handbook* see Reference below.

HUGHES introduction to edition, see Annotated editions above.

KNIGHT, G. WILSON 'The frozen labyrinth: an essay on M' *The burning oracle* 1939.

LEAVIS, F. R. 'M's verse' *Revaluation* 1936 repr *M's epic poetry* ed Patrides 1967.

MACCAFFREY, ISABEL G. *PL as myth* 1959.

PATRIDES, C. A. ed *Approaches to PL: the York tercentenary lectures* 1968. 13 lectures, some separately noted here.

ed *M's epic poetry: essays on PL and PR* with an annotated reading list 1967. Many separately noted here.

RAJAN, B. *PL and the 17c reader* 1947. Ch on style repr *M's epic poetry* ed Patrides.

RICKS, CHRISTOPHER *M's grand style* Oxford 1963. A ch repr *M's epic poetry* ed Patrides.

SEWELL, ARTHUR *A study in M's Christian doctrine* 1939.

SHAWCROSS, JOHN T. 'The style and genre of *PL*' in *New essays on PL* ed Thos. Kranidas, Berkeley 1969.

SHUMAKER, WAYNE *Unpremeditated verse: feeling and perception in M's PL* Princeton 1969.

SITWELL, EDITH *The pleasures of poetry* 1930.

STEIN, ARNOLD *Answerable style: essays on PL* Minneapolis 1953. Ch repr *M's epic poetry* ed Patrides.

SUMMERS, JOSEPH H. *The muse's method: an introduction to PL* 1962. Chs repr *M's epic poetry* ed Patrides and *Milton, PL: a collection of critical essays* ed L. L. Martz 1966.

'The embarrassments of *PL*' *Approaches to PL* ed Patrides 1968.

TILLYARD, E. M. W. *Milton* 1930 rev 1966.

WALDOCK, A. J. A. *PL and its critics* Cambridge 1947. Ch on the fall repr *M's epic poetry* ed Patrides.

WATKINS, W. B. C. *An anatomy of M's verse* Baton Rouge 1955. Ch on creation repr *M: modern essays in criticism* ed A. E. Barker 1965.

PL topics

See also introductions to individual books of the poem. *PMLA = Publications of the Modern Language Association* of America.

ALLEN, DON CAMERON 'Description as cosmos: the visual image in *PL*' *The harmonious vision: studies in M's poetry* Baltimore 1954.

BELL, MILLICENT 'The fallacy of the fall in *PL*' *PMLA* LXVIII 1953 863–83 and subsequently. See Shumaker below.

BODKIN, MAUD *Archetypal patterns in poetry: psychological studies of imagination* 1934. Jungian psychology, especially on Satan.

BROADBENT, J. B. 'M's rhetoric' *Modern Philology* LVI 1959 repr *Modern judgements: M* ed A. Rudrum 1968.

EMPSON, WILLIAM '"All" in *PL*' *The structure of complex words* 1951.

FOWLER, ALASTAIR Introduction to Carey and Fowler's edition listed above in Annotated editions section. Chronology, cosmology.

KERMODE, FRANK 'Adam unparadised' *The living M* ed Kermode 1960.

LAWRY, JON S. *The shadow of heaven* Ithaca N.Y. 1968.

LE COMTE, E. S. *Yet once more: verbal and psychological pattern in M* 1953.

LAWALSKI, BARBARA K. 'Structure and the symbolism of vision in Michael's prophecy, *PL* XI–XII' *Philological Quarterly* XLII 1936 25–35.

LODGE, ANN 'Satan's syndrome: a psychological interpretation of M's Satan' *Psychoanalytical Review* XLIII 1956 411–22.

LOVEJOY, A. O. 'M and the paradox of the fortunate fall'. Repr in his *Essays in the history of ideas* Baltimore 1948 and *M's epic poetry* ed Patrides 1967.

PRINCE, F. T. 'On the last two books of *PL*' *Essays and Studies* of the English Association 1958.

RADZINOWICZ, MARY ANN 'Man as a probationer of immortality: *PL* XI–XII' *Approaches to PL* ed Patrides 1968.

ROSS, MALCOLM M. *M's royalism: the conflict of symbol and idea in the poems* Ithaca N.Y. 1943.

'M and the protestant aesthetic' *Univ of Toronto Quarterly* XVII 1948 repr in his *Poetry and dogma* 1954 1969.

SAMUEL, IRENE 'The dialogue in heaven: a reconsideration of *PL* III 1–47' *PMLA* LXXII 1957 601–11.

'*PL* as mimesis' *Approaches to PL* ed Patrides 1968.

SAURAT, DENIS *M, man and thinker* 1924 rev 1944.

SHUMAKER, WAYNE 'The fallacy of the fall in *PL*' *PMLA* LXX 1955 1185–1202. See Bell above.

SUMMERS, JOSEPH H. '"Grateful vicissitude" in *PL*' *PMLA* LXIX 1954 251–64.

SVENDSEN, KESTER 'Adam's soliloquy in *PL* x' *College English* X 1949 366–70 repr *M: modern essays in criticism* ed A. E. Barker 1965.

WHALER, JAMES 'The compounding and distribution of similes in *PL*' *Modern Philology* XXVIII 1931 313–27.
'The Miltonic simile' *PMLA* XLVI 1931 1034–74.

WIDMER, KINGSLEY 'The iconography of renunciation: the Miltonic simile' *Journal of English Literary History* XXV 1958 258–69 repr *M's epic poetry* ed Patrides 1967.

Sources and composition of PL

GILBERT, ALAN H. *On the composition of PL: a study of the ordering and insertion of material* Chapel Hill N.C. 1947.

McCOLLEY, GRANT *PL: an account of its growth and major origins, with a discussion of M's use of sources and literary patterns* Chicago 1940.

Illustrations to PL

The most important illustrated editions are, in chronological order, with artist's name first:

MEDINA, JOHN BAPTIST DE *PL* 4th ed 1688. The frontispiece of Satan rousing the fallen angels has a surrealist air.

CHERON, LOUIS and THORNHILL, SIR JAMES *Poetical works* 2 vols 1720.

HAYMAN, FRANCIS *PL* ed T. Newton 2 vols 1749.

WESTALL, J. *Poetical works* with life by W. Hayley 3 vols 1794–7.

FUSELI, HENRY and HAMILTON, W. engraved by F. Bartolozzi. *PL* 2 vols 1802.

BLAKE, WILLIAM See *PL by JM: illustrations by WB* Liverpool (Lyceum Press) 1906; Darrell Figgis ed *The paintings of WB* 1925; *Poems in English by JM with illustrations by WB* ed H. C. Beeching and Geoffrey Keynes 2 vols (Nonesuch Press) 1926; C. H. Collins Baker *Exhibition of WB's watercolor drawings of M's PL* San Marino, California 1936 (for Huntington Library, where one of the two extant sets of originals is held); *PL illustrated by WB* New York (Heritage Press) 1940.

MARTIN, JOHN *The PL of JM with illustrations designed and engraved by John Martin* 2 vols 1827.

TURNER, J. M. W. *Poetical works* ed Sir E. Brydges 6 vols 1835.

FLATTERS, J. J. *The PL of M: translated into 54 designs by JJF* 1843.

DELMOTTE, W. A. *Drawings to M's PL* 1856. 474 plates.

DORÉ, GUSTAVE *M's PL* ed R. Vaughan 1866.

JOUBERT, F. *PL by JM* 1879. 38 illustrations including 4 engraved by FJ.

See C. H. COLLINS BAKER 'Some illustrators of M's *PL* (1688–1850)' *Library* 5th series III 1948–9 1–21 and 101–19 corrected by THOMAS BALSTROM in IV 1949 146–7; and MARCIA R. POINTER *M and English art* Manchester 1970.

Art and iconography

The best start is to make a careful study of Michelangelo's paintings of creation, fall and flood, and the supporting Biblical–classical figures, on the Sistine Chapel ceiling. That work alone, with a commentary, is more than adequate as a visual background to *PL*. His *Last judgement*, on the altar wall, may be compared with Rodin's sculpture *The gates of hell*.

If you want to go further, work outwards from Michelangelo with a renaissance picturebook and some illustrated editions of the following painters.

Going backwards towards the middle ages, see Adam and Eve studies by GHIBERTI (in bronze relief on the Baptistry doors, Florence), MASACCIO (expulsion), JACOPO DELLA QUERCIA (carved expulsions), JAN VAN EYCK (Ghent altarpiece *c.* 1430); the surrealist hells and paradises of HIERONYMUS BOSCH; and P. d'Ancona and E. Aeschlimann *The art of illumination: an anthology of MSS from the 6th to the 16th century* 1969. Going forwards:

RAPHAEL 1483–1520 especially 3 paintings in the Stanza della Segnatura, Vatican: *Adam and Eve* being tempted by an Eve-headed serpent; *The school of Athens* for a renaissance view of Socrates, Plato and others as quasi-divine dignitaries; and *Parnassus* for Apollo and the Muses, Dante, Ariosto etc. (cf. Poussin).

TINTORETTO 1518–94 *Creation of the animals, Last judgement* and *Adam and Eve* all in Venice; *Battle between Michael and Satan* Dresden.

BRUEGEL (Pieter B. the elder) 1525?–1569 *The fall of the rebel angels* at Brussels has un-Miltonic figures. *Dulle Griet* (Mad Meg) at Antwerp has a fearsome head of Satan.

RUBENS 1577–1640 Two pictures of *The fall of the angels* (or *the damned*) at Munich. Many paintings illustrate the fleshly frenzy that M opposed, e.g. *Bacchanal* in the Hermitage, Leningrad; and see *Judgement of Paris* in National Gallery London. His *Fall* (Hague) presents Adam and Eve as part of the world of animals and vegetables.

POUSSIN 1594–1665. A literary painter, e.g. *Parnassus* in the Prado, Madrid (cf. Raphael) and *Inspiration of the epic poet* (Louvre). A polished, classical sensuality in *The nurture of Jupiter* (Dulwich), *The triumph of Neptune* (Philadelphia) – worth pages of footnotes on classical allusion. Giants and airborne gods acclimatized in *A dance to the music of time* (Wallace collection, London), *Landscape with Polyphemus* (Hermitage, Leningrad), *Landscape with Orion* (Metropolitan N.Y.). Magnificently credible God with cherubim in *Miracle of St Francis Xavier* (Louvre) and *Moses and the burning bush* (Copenhagen). Chief *PL* work: *The earthly paradise* and *The flood* in a quartet called *The four seasons* (Louvre).

BERNINI 1598–1680 sculptor and architect, useful for tensely sculpted classical subjects, e.g. *Pluto and Proserpine* and *Apollo and Daphne* in Galleria Borghese, Rome, *Neptune and Triton* (Victoria and Albert, London). His 'glory' above the throne in St Peter's, Rome, is a three-dimensional version of the 17c concept of heaven.

To study a particular topic such as angels, the Three Graces, pictures of buildings, it is best to start with a book that covers a wide range such as

KENNETH CLARK *The nude* or BERNARD BERENSON *The Italian painters of the renaissance*. For other topics, and art history generally, see:

COLLINS BAKER, C. H. and W. G. CONSTABLE *English painting of the 16th and 17th centuries* Florence and Paris 1930.

DIDRON, ADOLPHE NAPOLÉON *Christian iconography; or the history of Christian art in the middle ages* trans E. J. Millington, rev M. Stokes 2 vols 1896 Bohn's library.

FERGUSON, GEO. *Signs and symbols in Christian art with illustrations from paintings of the renaissance* 1954 etc.

HUYGHE, RÉNÉ ed *Larousse encyclopedia of renaissance and baroque art* 1944.

PLUMB, J. H. ed *The Horizon book of the renaissance* 1961 repr as *The Penguin* etc. 1964.

SHEARMAN, JOHN *Mannerism* 1967.

TRAPP, J. B. 'The iconography of the fall of man' *Approaches to PL* ed C. A. Patrides 1968. Illustrated.

WIND, EDGAR *Pagan mysteries in the renaissance* 1958 rev 1967.

WÖLFFLIN, HEINRICH *Renaissance and baroque* trans K. Simon 1964.

A book of emblems such as FRANCIS QUARLES *Emblems* 1635 etc. with editions by G. Gilfillan 1857, W. W. Wilkins 1859 and A. B. Grosart (*Collected works* 3 vols 1880–1); or see the ceiling of the gallery at Blickling Hall, near Aylsham, Norfolk (National Trust): its plaster panels show in relief the emblems printed in HENRY PEACHAM *Minerva Britanna or a garden of heroical devices furnished and adorned with emblems and impresas of sundry natures newly devised, moralised and published in 1612*. Another practical approach is HENRY GREEN *Shakespeare and the emblem writers* 1870.

The Victoria and Albert Museum, Cromwell Road – Exhibition Road, London S.W. 7, South Kensington Underground, open free 10 (Sunday 2.30) to 6, is the most civilized museum in the world. A little time spent there is the most economical introduction not just to the iconography of *PL* but to the poem as a whole, and to western culture. Look at specific things. Don't wander. If you go in a group, let pairs confine themselves to one material or room or topic. For a visit, stay on the lower floors and don't attempt more than the rooms devoted to EARLY MEDIEVAL ART, GOTHIC ART (briskly) and parts of RENAISSANCE: ITALY and HIGH RENAISSANCE. In the earlier rooms aim, for example, at:

Byzantine ivories illustrating classical and Christian myths together, in relief.

South Italian walnut column with capital carving of Adam and Eve; cf. Dürer's engraving of them; and Loy Hering's homely yet classical version (16th-century German).

Alton Tower triptych for typology.

Angels embroidered on English and German chasubles.

Film and TV

See SERGEI EISENSTEIN on the cinematic possibilities of *PL* in *The film sense* trans J. Layda 1943. His advice to use *PL* as 'a first-rate school in which to study montage and audio-visual relationships' has not been followed by professionals but could be by amateurs. It would probably involve much model constructing, and lighting.

Parts of *PL* have been used as accompaniment on various educational TV programmes, notably III 326... against Michelangelo's *Last judgement* in the Sistine Chapel, with tuba, in a BBC Schools TV programme on Michelangelo in a series called *People of the renaissance* 1960, probably now wiped. Much remains to be done: e.g. the debate in Pandemonium is an opportunity for TV puppetry.

Speech

The chief recorded readings from *PL* are:

Books I–IV selections read by Anthony Quayle. Caedmon double TC-2008.
Books I, II selections, III–IV selections, V–VI selections, VII and IX selections,
  IX and X selections and end of XII read by various actors, mostly
  Cambridge based, under the direction of George Rylands (e.g. Tony
  Church, Michael Redgrave, Patrick Wymark). Argo 431, 432, 463, 464,
  508, 509, with texts provided.

These are theatrical readings. Better to spend the money on a tape-recorder and make your own. To make the lines sound right you have to discover what they mean. This process can be hastened by trying to add sound effects. They can be wiped later when the reading has been perfected.

Music and dance

Play and listen to the music of Henry Lawes (friend of M, wrote music for *Comus*, M wrote sonnet to him). For orchestral music, which developed in England along with opera about the time *PL* was published, the most relevant composers are Purcell (*c.* 1657–95), Vivaldi (*c.* 1675–1743), Handel (1685–1759) for oratorios, Bach (1685–1750) for fugues (see *PL* XI 552 and Crashaw's poem *Music's duel*) and Haydn (1732–1809) for oratorios including *Creation*. You might try making your own lost paradise music, either with a group or in concrete; cf. Desmond Leslie's *Death of Satan* in his *Musique concrète* disc MC 1001, originally composed for Ronald Duncan's play of that name on ABC TV and at the Royal Court Theatre, London.

There are suggestions for improvisations and dance in the section on myth and ritual. You might be able to find some material from Roland Petit's production of *PL* as a ballet at the Royal Opera House, Covent Garden, London, which opened 23 February 1967, with Margot Fonteyn and Rudolph Nureyev, music by Marius Constant.

HOLLANDER, JOHN *The untuning of the sky* Princeton 1961.
MORRIS, BRIAN '"Not without song": M and the composers' *Approaches to PL* ed C. A. Patrides 1968.
PATTISON, BRUCE *Music of the English renaissance* 1948.

Milton's influence

HAVENS, R. D. *The influence of M on English poetry* Cambridge Mass. 1922.

PARKER, W. R. *M's contemporary reputation* Columbus, Ohio 1940.

WASSERMAN, E. R. 'Early evidences of M's influence' *Modern Language notes* LVIII 1943.

Literary history

CRUTTWELL, PATRICK *The Shakespearean moment and its place in the poetry of the 17c* 1954.

DAY, MARTIN S. *History of English literature to 1660* and *1660–1837* 1963. Doubleday college course guides. Businesslike.

FAIRCHILD, H. N. *Religious trends in English poetry* vols I–III New York 1939 1942 1949.

FORD, BORIS gen ed *Pelican guides to English literature*. Introductory and background chapters.

GARNET, RICHARD and GOSSE, EDMUND *English literature: an illustrated record* 4 vols 1903. Copiously illustrated. Unsurpassed.

McLUHAN, MARSHALL *Understanding media: the extensions of man* 1964. Especially chs. 8–11 and 18 on words and numbers.

MILES, JOSEPHINE *Eras and modes in English poetry* 1957 2nd ed Berkeley and L.A. 1964. Linguistic criteria.

ROSS, MALCOLM M. *Poetry and dogma: the transfiguration of eucharistic symbols in 17c English poetry* New Brunswick 1954 New York 1969.

SYPHER, WYLIE *Four stages of renaissance style: transformations in art and literature 1400–1700* 1955.

Epic and mythology

CAMPBELL, JOSEPH *The hero with a thousand faces* 1949 etc.

CANDELARIA, F. and STRANGE, W. C. ed *Perspectives on epic* 1969.

COOK, ELIZABETH *The ordinary and the fabulous: an introduction to myths, legends and fairy tales for teaching and storytelling* Cambridge 1969.

ELIADE, MIRCEA *The myth of the eternal return* trans W. R. Trask 1954.

FLETCHER, ANGUS *Allegory: the theory of a symbolic mode* Ithaca, New York 1964.

FRYE, NORTHROP *Fables of identity: studies in poetic mythology* 1963. Section I on archetypes, myth, Homer.

GRANSDEN, K. W. '*PL* and the *Aeneid*' *Essays in Criticism* XVII 1967 281–303.

GREENE, THOS. M. *The descent from heaven* New Haven 1963. Epic.

HARDING, DAVIS P. *The club of Hercules: studies in the classical background of PL* Evanston 1962.

HIGHET, GILBERT H. *The classical tradition: Greek and Roman influences on western literature* 1949.

LEACH, EDMUND *Genesis as myth and other essays* 1969.

SCHUMAKER, WAYNE *Literature and the irrational: a study in anthropological backgrounds* 1960.

TILLYARD, E. M. W. *The English epic and its background* 1954.
WILLEY, BASIL chapters on the difficulties of divine epic for M in *The 17c background*.

Religion

See Hastings in the Reference section below and works on the reformation in History. There is no substitute for (a) reading the Bible, especially the early chapters of *Genesis*, the poetical chapters of *Job* on the creator's might (e.g. xxx ff.), *Psalms*, *Solomon's Song*, parts of *Isaiah* (e.g. xlv ff.), the early chapters of *John*, *Romans* (especially viii), *Revelation* (especially xix ff.); (b) attending worship in Roman Catholic and Anglican churches and the meeting of a dissenting sect (as low as possible).

CHADWICK, OWEN *The reformation* 1965 Pelican history of the church vol III.
DONNE, JOHN *Sermons: selected* by L. P. Smith, Oxford 1919; or Jeremy Taylor's prose.
ERIKSON, ERIK H. *Young man Luther: a study in psychoanalysis and history* 1959
MILTON, JOHN *Of reformation touching church discipline in England: and the causes that hitherto have hindered it* 1641; *The reason of church government urged against prelaty* 1642; *De doctrina christiana* (*Of Christian doctrine*, not published till 1825). See editions of Hughes and Patterson cited above. The most convenient British edition of the prose is still *The prose works of JM* ed J. A. St John in Bohn's standard library 5 vols 1848, not too difficult to get second hand.
SANTAYANA, GEORGE The poetry of Christian dogma in his *Interpretations of poetry and religion*.
SEWELL, ARTHUR *A study in M's Christian doctrine* 1939. Sympathetic and perceptive relating of *De doctrina christiana* to the poetry.

History of ideas, science, Weltanschauung

There is no substitute for careful study of E. M. W. TILLYARD *The Elizabethan world-picture* 1943 and JAMES WINNY ed *The frame of order: an outline of Elizabethan belief taken from treatises of the late 16c* 1957, accelerated by visual material (see section on art).

BROCKBANK, PHILIP ' "Within the visible diurnal sphere": the moving world of *PL*' *Approaches to PL* ed C. A. Patrides 1968.
BUSH, DOUGLAS *The renaissance and English humanism* Toronto 1939.
DONNE, JOHN *Anniversaries* ed F. Manley 1963.
FREUD, SIGMUND *Civilisation and its discontents* trans Joan Rivière 1929. *Collected papers* trans Rivière 1925 especially vols 4 and 5.
GRACE, WILLIAM *Ideas in M* 1968.
HAYDN, HIRAM K. *The counter-renaissance* 1950.
JONES, ERNEST 'The God complex' and 'A psychoanalytic study of the Holy Ghost' *Essays in applied psychoanalysis* 1923.
LOVEJOY, A. O. *The great chain of being: a study in the history of an idea* Cambridge Mass. 1936.

166

MARCUSE, HERBERT *Eros and civilisation: a philosophical inquiry into Freud* 1956. Especially chs. 8–11.
NICOLSON, MARJORIE H. 'M and the telescope' *English literary history* II 1935.
RHYS, H. H. ed *17c science and the arts* Princeton 1961.
SVENDSEN, KESTER *M and Science* Cambridge Mass. 1956.
TILLYARD as above.
WHITEHEAD, A. N. *Adventures of ideas* Cambridge 1947. Cosmologies etc.
WILLEY, BASIL *The 17c background: studies of the thought of the age in relation to poetry and religion* 1934.
WINNY as above.

Geography

Study a contemporary atlas of the world, e.g. Gerard Mercator *Historia mundi or Mercator's atlas* trans W. Saltonstall 1635 *et seq.* (original 1595), or Abraham Ortelius *Theatrum orbis terrarum* Antwerp 1570, published as *The theatre of the world* 1608, or Jodocus Hondius the elder *Christian knight map of the world* 1597, rare, copy in British Museum, repr with article by Amy Lee Turner in *Milton newsletter* III ii May 1969 pp. 26–30. All these maps have emblematic decorations which run not only to mermaids and whales but to serious representations of such items as the last judgement, Adam and Eve, Sin and Death; they can be more instructive about 17c ideas than many chapters of intellectual history books.

HEYLYN, PETER *Cosmography* 1652. World travel. Easier to manage than Hakluyt or Purchas.
SANDYS, GEORGE *Relation of a journey*...(to the middle east) 1610. As a verse paraphraser of the Bible he noticed a good deal about Palestine that is significant for *PL*.

History

A short selection slanted for *PL*.

ASHLEY, MAURICE *Life in Stuart England* 1964 rev 1967.
BETHELL, S. L. *The cultural revolution of the 17c* 1951.
BROWN, NORMAN O. *Life against death: the psychoanalytical meaning of history* 1959.
BUSH, M. L. *Renaissance, reformation and the outer world* 1967.
DICKENS, A. G. *The English reformation* 1964.
FERGUSON, WALLACE K. *The renaissance* 1940.
KENYON, J. P. *The Stuarts: a study in English kingship* 1956. Illustrated.
PLUMB, J. H. ed *The Horizon book of the renaissance* 1961 repr as *The Penguin* etc. 1967.
SMITH, DAVID NICHOL ed *Characters of the 17c* Oxford 1918. Contemporary accounts of over 60 great men including Milton, Cromwell, the kings and some bishops.
SOLA, PINTO V. DE *The English renaissance 1510–1688* 1938. Excellent historical chapters in this literary history, and bibliography.
STONE, LAWRENCE *The crisis of the aristocracy 1558–1641* 1965, abridged 1967.

TAWNEY, R. H. *Religion and the rise of capitalism* 1926.
TAYLOR, G. RATTRAY *Sex in history* 1953 rev 1959.
TREVELYAN, G. M. *England under the Stuarts* 1904.
WEDGWOOD, C. V. *The great rebellion:* vol I *The King's peace* 1955; II *The King's war* 1958.
Milton and his world 1969. Illustrated.
WRIGHT, LOUIS B. *Middle-class culture in Elizabethan England* 1935. Mainly on popular literature; relevant to 17c also.
WEBER, MAX *The protestant ethic and the spirit of capitalism* trans T. Parsons 1930.
Thames and Hudson are now issuing a series called 'Ancient People and Places' which is in the good tradition of Victorian illustrated books. It contains several relevant volumes, e.g. Aldred *The Egyptians*, Harden *The Phoenicians*, Gray *The Canaanites*, Smail *The Crusaders*, Oates *Babylon*.

Reference

BRADSHAW, JOHN ed *Concordance to the poetical works of JM* 1894.
Brewer's dictionary of phrase and fable. Many editions since 1870.
DAVIDSON, GUSTAV ed *Dictionary of angels, including the fallen angels* 1967.
HANFORD, J. H. and TAAFE, J. G. *A Milton handbook* 5th rev edition 1969 (avoid earlier editions, going back to 1926).
HASTINGS, JAMES ed *Dictionary of the Bible* 5 vols Edinburgh and New York 1898. Many lesser works also available.
ed *Encyclopaedia of religion and ethics* 13 vols 1908–27.
SKEAT, W. W. and MAYHEW, A. L. *A glossary of Tudor and Stuart words, especially from the dramatists* 1914.
The shorter Oxford English dictionary 2 vols 1933, 3rd ed 1944 etc.
WILLIAMSON, MARGARET *Colloquial language of the Commonwealth and Restoration* English Association pamphlet no. 73 Oxford 1929.

Bibliography

Most helpful is the *Annotated reading list* appended to *M's epic poetry: essays on PL and PR* ed C. A. Patrides (Penguin) 1967. It could be kept up to date by subscribing to the *Milton quarterly* issued since 1967 from the English Dept., Ohio University, Athens, Ohio 45701, U.S.A. This contains abstracts and reviews of current work. The standard annual list is *Recent literature of the English renaissance* in *Studies in philology* spring issues since April 1923. J. H. Hanford's *Milton* in the Goldentree bibliographies series (general ed O. B. Hardison Jr.), New York 1966, is slanted in the other direction from the booklist you are reading now; so are the lists in M. Y. Hughes's paperback edition of *PL*, Odyssey Press, New York 1962 (books since 1934, editions since 1935, articles and unpublished dissertations since 1957). Most annotated editions contain booklists. It is often best to start from an item referred to in a footnote in a book, though.

Annotated editions of PL

LE COMTE, E. S. ed *PL and other poems by JM* [*Samson, Lycidas*] 1961 Mentor. Modernized text, judicious notes.

PL general

BLAMIRES, HARRY *M's creation: a guide through PL* 1971.

BROADBENT, J. B. and LORNA SAGE a cassette-recorded discussion of *PL* (and other peoms by M) in preparation: for distribution by Sussex Tapes 1971.

RUDDUCK, JEAN a portfolio of loose-leaf materials, verbal and graphic, to serve as texts for the discussion and elucidation of various *PL* topics: in preparation 1971.

PL topics

BRIGGS, KATHARINE M. *Pale Hecate's team: an examination of the beliefs in witchcraft and magic among Shakespeare's contemporaries and his immediate successors* 1962. One way in to the study of Satan.

Music and dance

I should have recommended Girolamo Frescobaldi, organist of St Peter's, Rome, 1608–28. Some of his work was broadcast from an organ in Corsica on BBC3 in 1971.

Hungarian stage adaptation of *PL* by Karoly Kazimir at the Thalia Theatre, Budapest, July 1970, noticed in *Milton quarterly* v March 1971 pp. 16–17.

Literary history

PMLA LXXXV 1970 devoted to 17c topics.

Epic and mythology

DOUGLAS, MARY *Natural symbols: explorations in cosmology* 1970. 'Grid and group' anthropology, some of it closely related to *PL* topics.

RADICE, BETTY ed *Who's who in the ancient world* 1971. A classical dictionary extending into a guide to the modern uses made of ancient materials.

Chronology of Bible, hexaëmera, epic, PL etc

See chapters on myth, epic, and the publication of *PL*, above.

BC

1230	Exodus of children of Israel from Egypt. Trojan war.
c. 1000	David, Solomon. Homer.
c. 750	Isaiah fl.
640	Josiah's reformation; Jeremiah fl.
586	Jews exiled to Babylon; Ezekiel fl.
c. 536	Jews return from Babylonian exile.
c. 500	Aeschylus (Greek tragedy).
5th cent	Canon of Jewish law and prophets established.
399	Socrates executed; Plato fl.
327	Alexander the Great in India; battle of the Hydaspes; Hellenistic civilization. Founding of Rome.
55	Julius Caesar invades Celtic Britain.
31	Antony and Cleopatra commit suicide. Virgil, Horace, Catullus, Ovid fl.
BC – AD	Apocrypha and pseudepigrapha providing Hellenistic elaborations of OT myth, e.g. *Enoch*.

AD

c. 33	Crucifixion.
1st cent	Philo Judaeus (a Hellenistic Jew of Alexandria) *Account of the world's creation* (reconciles Moses' account in *Genesis* with Plato's in his *Timaeus*) – Greek.
4th cent	St Basil, bishop of Caesarea *Hexameron* – account of paradise and the fall – Greek. St Ambrose, bishop of Milan, treatise on *Genesis* – Latin. (Ambrose was famous for being able to read silently.)
c. 400	St Augustine, bishop of Hippo, commentary on *Genesis* and other exegesis of the fall, original sin etc. – Latin. Prudentius (a Christian Spaniard at the imperial court in Rome) *Hamartigenia* and *Psychomachia*, poems on Satan versus the soul – Latin. Knowledge of Greek lost in western Europe.
8th cent	Caedmon MS *Genesis A* and *B*, *Exodus* etc. *Beowulf* – Anglo-Saxon.
1096	First Crusade.
12th cent	Shift of attention to New Testament, saints, Virgin; shift of form to lyric, drama. Plastic treatment of Adam and Eve and of hell in sculpture and MS illumination.

14th cent	Mystery plays begin.
	Dante *Divina commedia* – Italian.
	Renaissance painting in Italy.
15th cent	Recovery of Greek in western Europe. Ambrose and Basil published 1490 and 1532 with prefaces by Erasmus. Scientific speculation. Shift of attention to the fall, sin etc. Heroic motives of exploration, colonial expansion, nationalism.
1472	Cornozano *Discorso in versi della creazione del mondo*.
1480	Caxton trans and printed *Mirror of the world* from Gossouin *Image du monde* 1245 – popular encyclopedia of universe, creation and fall, angels etc.
1508–20	Michelangelo paints ceiling of Vatican chapel with scenes of creation, fall, flood etc. Raphael paints walls of Vatican rooms with Old and New Testament and classical subjects.
1527	Vida *Christiad* – Latin epic by Italian writer; influential treatment of hell. Last English mystery plays written about now.
1532	Ariosto *Orlando furioso* – Italian romantic epic on Charlemagne and Roland v the Moors.
1500–50	Luther, Calvin: reformation theology, including commentaries on *Genesis* and discussions of original sin.
1568	Alfani *Battaglia celeste tra Michele e Lucifero*.
1572	Camoens *Os Lusiads* – Portuguese epic.
1576	Tasso *Gerusalemme liberata* 1st edition – Italian romantic epic on Crusades.
1578	Du Bartas *La sepmaine ou création* – French.
c. 1580	Camoens *Da creacaõ e composicaõ do homen*.
1584	Du Bartas *La seconde sepmaine* – history of man.
1589–96	Spenser *Fairy Queen*.
1590	Valvasone *L'angeleida* – epic on war in heaven; invention of cannon introduced.
1591	Harington trans Ariosto *Orlando furioso*.
1592–99	Sylvester trans Du Bartas as *Divine weeks and works*.
1593	Tasso *Gerusalemme liberata* 2nd edition allegorized.
1600	Fairfax trans Tasso as *Godfrey of Boulogne*.
1601	Grotius *Adamus exul* – Latin tragedy; Netherlands.
1605–15	Cervantes *Don Quixote* – Spanish mock romance.
1607	Tasso *Le sette giornate del mondo creato* – Italian blank verse imitating Du Bartas.
1613	Andreini *Adamo* – lyric drama of the kind M saw in Italy; repr 1617, 1641.
	Chapman trans Homer *Iliad* and *Odyssey*.
1620s	Quarles, Sandys: verse paraphrases of *Job*, *Samson* etc. Lancelot Andrewes sermons on *Genesis*. G. Fletcher poems on Christ as hero.
1630s	Donne and Herbert poems published. Emblem books flourished.
1638	M in Italy.
1640–42	M planning divine tragedies, British tragedies and epics.
1650	Davenant *Gondibert* with preface; and Hobbes's answer.
1654	Vondel *Lucifer* – Netherlands; political drama.
	M writing *PL*.

1655	Fanshawe trans Camoens *The Lusiads*.
1656	Cowley *Davideis* with preface.
1664	Vondel *Adam in Ballingschap* – Dutch lyrical drama on marriage, temptation and fall of Adam and Eve.
1667	*Paradise lost*. Sprat *History of the Royal Society*.
1671	*Paradise regained; Samson agonistes*.
1674	*Paradise lost* 2nd edition with Marvell's poem.
1677	Dryden *State of innocence* – operatic version of *PL*.
1678	*PL* 3rd edition.
1688	*PL* 4th edition folio by subscription with Dryden's lines and Medina's illustrations.
1695	*PL* 6th edition (and other poems bound in) with notes by Patrick Hume. Sir Richard Blackmore *Prince Arthur: a heroic poem* – Arthur's enemies are agents of Lucifer; includes Thor and Odin, angels, creation and fall.
1697	Dryden trans Virgil *Aeneid*. Charles Perrault *Adam, ou la création de l'homme, sa chute et sa reparation: poème chrestien*.
1712	Addison's essays on *PL* in *Spectator*. Blackmore *Creation* – didactic epic.
1726	Pope trans Homer *Iliad* and *Odyssey*.
1730s	Pope *Essay on man* – didactic. *Dunciad* – mock-epic.
1732	Bentley ed *PL*.
1733	Pearce's notes on *PL*.
1734	Richardsons' notes on *PL*.
c. 1740	Handel *Samson* – oratorio of *SA*.
1749	Newton ed Milton's poems.
1757	F. G. Klopstock *Der Tod Adams* – prose tragedy on Adam and his sons. Considerable interest from now on in Cain and Abel rather than the fall.
c. 1770	Goethe *Prometheus* – German poem.
1779	Johnson *Lives of the most eminent English poets*.
c. 1793	Blake *Marriage of heaven and hell*.
1798	Haydn *Creation* – oratorio. Coleridge *The wanderings of Cain* – prose poem.
1804–08	Blake *Milton*.
1805	Wordsworth *Prelude*.
1808	Goethe *Faust* part 1 – German drama.
1817	Mary Shelley *Frankenstein* – Gothic novel reworking *PL*.
1818	Shelley *Revolt of Islam*.
1819	Byron *Don Juan* cantos i and ii.
1820	Keats *Hyperion*. Shelley *Prometheus unbound*.
1821	Byron *Cain: a mystery*. Maturin *Melmoth the wanderer* – cf. 1817.
1830	Robert Montgomery *Satan: a poem*.
1844	Elizabeth B. Browning *A drama of exile* – verse drama on Adam and Eve. Kierkegaard *The concept of dread* (excerpts by Auden 1955).

1853   Arnold *Sohrab and Rustum.*
c. 1855   Victor Hugo *La fin de Satan* – he is eventually regenerated.
1859   Victor Hugo *Le sacre de la femme* – Eden and Eve, especially her emotions and pregnancy, before the fall. *La conscience* – Cain.
1859–72   Tennyson *Idylls of the king.*
1865   Christina Rossetti *Eve* – mourning for Abel.
1880   G. M. Hopkins *Spring and fall.*
1888   Hermann Melville *Billy Budd, foretopman* – hero as Adam and Christ; published 1924, opera.
1899   George Santayana *Lucifer or the heavenly truce: a theological tragedy* – verse drama in which Lucifer's love for Hermes shows him to be 'an atheistical saint'.
1901   G. B. Shaw *Man and superman.*
1904   Laurence Binyon *The death of Adam.*
1908   Charles Doughty *Adam cast forth* – prose drama in archaic diction.
       Henri Barbusse *L'enfer* – hell revealed in a hotel room.
1916   James Joyce *A portrait of the artist as a young man* – section 3, sermon on sin and hell.
1921   Shaw *Back to Methusaleh.*
       Joyce *Ulysses.*
       Eliot *Waste land.*
1937   Charles Williams *Descent into hell* – novel; see below.
1941   Reinhold Niebuhr *The nature and destiny of man: a Christian interpretation* – neo-reformation theology; cf. Brunner, Barth.
1942   W. H. Auden *Hymn to St Cecilia*, music by Benjamin Britten (Opus 27) – Kierkegaardian theology.
1943   C. S. Lewis *Perelandra* (re-issued as *Voyage to Venus* 1960) – Garden of Eden re-enacted.
1945   C. S. Lewis *That hideous strength: a modern fairytale for grown-ups.*
       Jean-Paul Sartre *Huis clos* (previously *Les autres*; trans S. Gilbert as *In camera* 1946) – play about self-inflicted hell, the vicious circle.
1946   Paul Valéry *Lust, la demoiselle de cristal*, in his *Mon Faust* – bitter comedy: Faust tempted in an Eden.
1947   Chas. Williams *Many dimensions*; *War in heaven.*
1951   Sartre *Le diable et le bon Dieu* trans K. Black as *Lucifer and the Lord* 1952.
1954   William Golding *Lord of the flies* – original sin; title = Beelzebub.
       J. R. Tolkien *The lord of the rings* – prose epic on conflict between good and evil.
1955   Golding *The inheritors.*
1956   Edwin Muir *Adam's dream, The fall* etc. in *One foot in Eden.*
       Albert Camus *La chute* (The fall) – novel.
1957   Samuel Beckett *All that fall: a play for radio.*
1959   Golding *Free fall* – Dantesque inquiry into sin.
       C. S. Lewis *The lion, the witch and the wardrobe* – allegory of atonement.

173

Contents of PL with some cross-references

See also chapter on Structures, above.

Paradise Lost
Introduction

JOHN BROADBENT
Professor of English Literature
University of East Anglia

In this, the first introductory volume of the new Cambridge
Milton for Schools and Colleges, Professor Broadbent, the general
editor of the series, presents background and introductory material
essential to today's student for a proper understanding of *PL*.
Chapters on mythology, the epic, the writing, publication and
subsequent editing of *PL*, and on Milton's ideology and world-view
provide the background to the poem as a whole. The second half of
the book engages with the poetry at a more detailed level, and
examines themes, structures, allusion, language, syntax, rhetoric,
similes, rhythm and style, always showing the reader how he can
best understand and appreciate Milton's usage. Extensive quotation
from *PL* and other works by Milton and others helps to make all
clear.

The volume is completed by a chronological table running from
1230 B.C. (Exodus of children of Israel from Egypt) to 1959 (publication of C. S. Lewis' *The lion, the witch and the wardrobe*) and a
list of the contents of *PL* with cross-references.

Cover illustration: The creation and fall of man, by Lorenzo Ghiberti.
Bronze panel from the East door of the Baptistry, Florence. Photo:
Mansell Collection.

CAMBRIDGE UNIVERSITY PRESS

London: Bentley House, 200 Euston Road, London NW1 2DB
New York: 32 East 57th Street, New York 10022
Melbourne: 296 Beaconsfield Parade, Middle Park, Victoria 3206
Sydney: 184 Sussex Street, Sydney, N.S.W. 2000

80p NET IN U.K. **$2.75** IN U.S.A. 0 521 09639 1

Also issued in cloth